Copyright © 2008 by Betty Hyland

ISBN 0-7414-5125-5

Published by:

INFI∞ITY
PUBLISHING.COM

1094 New DeHaven Street, Suite 100
West Conshohocken, PA 19428-2713
Info@buybooksontheweb.com
www.buybooksontheweb.com
Toll-free (877) BUY BOOK
Local Phone (610) 941-9999
Fax (610) 941-9959

Printed in the United States of America

Printed on Recycled Paper

Published December 2008

Childhood Memories

of the

Writers of Chantilly

Table of Contents

Who Are the Writers of Chantilly?

Twice a month we gather – people who have little in common, except a desire to write and who value one another's friendship and insight. Some are new and some have been together for years.

We write fiction, nonfiction, essays, poems. Each brings some expertise to the gathering in addition to a manuscript to be critiqued.

We are generous with our help – keenly, but kindly, critical of one another's work because we know there is nothing more uselessly critical than a rejection slip.

Some are veterans of three American wars who bring to their stories history and personal experience.

Some are young members who contribute enthusiasm, a sense of the modern, and a desire to learn the craft of writing.

Some have a story to tell that no one else could tell.

There are some who have endured terrible problems, or are trying to cope with them, or are about to face them and want to write in order to help others cope – or perhaps want to escape from their problems by writing mysteries or travel articles.

Not all members attend the meetings. Some now live out of state or out of the country, but are connected by that astonishing, vast network known as e-mail and are never far away. There are members who are shut-ins, write under pseudonyms, are too far away to drive, or have their own reasons. But most look forward to the next meeting.

When the meeting is over – and much too soon – we leave, often having no idea where the others live or work, what their personal lives are like. No one asks, unless the information is offered. When it is, it is held in confidence. So we say good-bye, get in our cars and drive away. We are like the dancers in "The Nutcracker Suite" who only appear on

1

Christmas Eve. We appear twice a month, then return to our mysterious, chaotic, or humdrum world enriched, encouraged, anxious to tell our stories.

Bitch Dance

By R. Patrick-Allister

RUING

Sitting on a park bench on Pennsylvania Ave. I look at the National Theatre sign. GISELLE. I feel nothing as I whisper the name to myself. Today is the last show. Sunday matinee. There is a ballet to dance. Today as Giselle, I am to love, to be beguiled and betrayed by my callous lover, to go mad, plunge a sword in my heart and die brokenhearted. But there is more for foolish peasant girls...As a forgiving, expansive spirit, I rise from my place of rest and save my undeserving love, Duke Albrecht, from his awaiting grave. When the generous deed is done, 1 waft down into my grave, alone but still in love. Just like a dumb girl.

The reviews from opening week are in my hands. "Giselle is danced with technical perfection, outstanding grace and lyricism" was but one rave. The words about me leave me unfazed and flat.

The day is bright and new. The slight wind stirs the falling leaves, tipped with shades of yellow, burnt ochre and brick red. I do not want to go in and work on my Pas de Deux. The sounds of nearby children playing and the raspy rustle of dry swirling leaves are simple and peaceful. So Giselle girl, this is it? The old scold echoes. Twenty-one hard years of nothing but ballet and now I am GISELLE. The audiences are now mine. The once caustic reviews now gush, their effusiveness embarrasses me. My dancing "draws and haunts" say one review. So, why do I feel tepid and unmoved? What is it I want? Fretting, I am restless with doubt, reproaching myself for being ungrateful. This is not the way I had planned it, not the way it was supposed to be.

BREAKING

My fiancé came into town to watch the show last night. He weighed me down, waxing tedious and intrusive. Pretending to be wild with want was belaboring; it was alien and wrong. Lounging in bed last night, I can still hear his milky voice drone on.

"I am a lucky guy. You are talented and sweet. You work hard. You are dedicated, dutiful and responsible." As if embarrassed, he whispered. "You are my very own goddess."

Inwardly wincing, I was soul-sick listening to what I looked like to the world. My insides churned, if only I could rage at him, shake him, body slam him across my threshold: Now stumble in, come in deeper pretty please and meet the others of me. This is Wild, Lashing Bitch. Here is Dark, Hungry Bitch. There is Vulgar, Slovenly Bitch. Over there is Raging, Scorching Bitch. So many of me, Sad, Empty, Restless, Yearning Bitches. One of the others of me fantasized raking his cheeks and slapping the simpering off his face. Of course, I only tamely smiled at him, meeking myself into a mousy silence. I tried not to implode as he snuggled closer and swished and fawned his hands up and down my back. Dark Bitch itched to break his manicured fingers. My swarm of bitches wept and wilted.

The fop left this morning; my relief was boundless. He walked away whistling into the roiling wind, his light coat gusting and billowing out. Watching him saunter away, I felt guiltless. Comforted, I knew there will be women in line for him. Maybe they can manicure together. Dull and listless, I turned away. He was one more thing that had gone wrong in my life. One more bland event to endure. With brutal resolve, I solemnly swore to break it off next week. G'bye pretty boy, Restless Bitch is checking out.

HURTING

Sitting in the park, I try to accept my unnamed sadness. I am changed. The unease started as thin whispers of discontent that niggled. Then grew. Now this loud unsettling loneliness clamors. What do I do with this abiding ache? Where do I put this hurt? What do I feed this hunger, it grows corrosive? Where do I slake this gaping thirst? Feeling small and bewildered, I sit lost in this big empty space of time. No tears. I won't cry. I wait for someone, something to come and crush me into their space. Come and slam into me, fight me, pound into me. Make me blisteringly alive. I crave edgy and hunger for a rage. Drag me from where I circle and circle. Drag me from where I crouch in the shadows. Do something, anything to stun and bite me. I look ahead. All I see is a long weeping into the dusk, into years. I wither at the thought, I grieve. Finally, I reluctantly rise and wend my way through the children and leaves into duty. After all, I am a professional.

ENDING

Ten minutes to show time. I check the creases of my flutter sleeves and run my hands over my pink and cream tutu of sheer georgette. Envisioning the orchestra, I hear them ready for the opening. They take their positions, starched and precise. I see the audience in my mind, the same wearying kind I am sure. They sally their wit and disguised barbs, they smile, tight and brittle. Gowned, aged women drip with glitter, genteel predators. Their staid men at tow. The younger act careless with blithe and blasé, but ever testing the thick undertow. All bandy, sleek and polished, hunkered down in money. I have to delight them, dance for them. Fleetingly, I wondered, when did I stop dancing for me? Closing my eyes, I steady myself and let their world swim away; the drift of timbered polite murmurs fades. The sea of faces looks on as the light dims. The plaintive wail of a sole violin arches high into the air. I let her in. I am the peasant girl Giselle, frail and beloved in this peaceful and sleepy hamlet. With the swooning of her heart, I am ready to love like her, to want for undying love. Gliding out, I am ready to die for love. I know it is my last ballet.

LEAVING

I pass on the party. I am done with slivers of twinkling, willowy ballerinas. To my drunken father, we merely flurried here and there on stage. A waste. Bitterly, I remember my father thinking of us as a feathery, wispy, useless lot. My years of searing physicality, of exhausting, punishing devotion and desire. He turns out to be right;, I am left passionless. Still wearing my ballet slippers and stage dress, I get into the rental car and drive out of town. My direction is nowhere.

Thinking of the dance, I drive. I had given the audience every piece of Giselle I could evoke. I danced to the mourning melody of lost love, stained and sundered by betrayal. I gave them my forlorn and tremulous tears. For them, I danced crazed and desolated by a dashed, romantic dream. Giselle's death was steeped in the most piercing agony I could give it. As I lowered into Giselle's grave, I cried. Not for Giselle. I cried for Sad, Empty Bitch.

I drive and drive. The day's muster and shimmer thins. Night is coming. The gossamer sky eases out the day. Bursts of orange swell high in the sky, streaked with molten reds. The low horizon, lace purple and violet. Skimming the earth, the day's deep sea blue and satin white slowly turns a muted gray. Beautiful. Serene. If only I can drive into the sky and mist into the last of deep sea blue and satin white. Road, take me all the way. Take me to the place I will sleep. Take me to the place that is everything. Drive on.

DYING

The miles roll smooth and carefree. The whooshing sound of tires lulls me into a space of dream. The lull shifts and grows uneasy. An insidious dread creeps up around me and burrows into my dream, stealthy and unholy. A voice breaks in. My voice. I hear myself in a shrill tone; I am demanding something...of God. I am in a coffin, the color of bleak and gone. My skin brushes against startling white velvet. Shrunken beings slink around my coffin. Powdery, bejeweled, sly women, squint down at me. Salacious, furtive men look at my nipples through the sheer gown. There are little girls, frilly ballerinas, they tip-toe to look at me. The girls try to reach for my hands to kiss, pursing little wet mauve lips. My fiancé comes. He is looking hard at my gaunt and lifeless face, tinged sallow and pinched. He grins, staring at my nipples.

He whispers, not embarrassed, "Nice to meet you, Dead Bitch."

Everybody shuffles off. I order God again. God, come here. Hold me. Blow warmth on my face and hands, they are cold. Where is my fire? It's too still, too quiet. God, who will I be now? What do I get to hanker for? Sinking into a cloud of black nothingness, I try not to falter and cry out, but I teeter on this edge of slow unfolding panic. I go over that edge. Giselle screams, trying to rip apart the air above. The crash of screams shred my throat and claw out of my chest. My face contorts and twists. But my screams are silent, eerily mute and empty, no sound pummels against the air. Spent and helpless I stop breathing and beseeching. The float down slurs long, murky and icy. It feels infinitely and intensely sad. It goes on and on. A ghastly freeze sets in, the silence deafens and death engulfs me. The depths moan and close in.

LIVING

I breathe. Wrenching for air, I am jarred alive. "See ya, Dead Bitch." Out of my vague haziness, I shudder off the murk and ice. Shaking, I am crisply, gloriously alive. A long time passes before my ragged gulps of air calm down. Looking around outside, I see fields stretch out in the darkening, whispering gloam. I get out of my car and my ballet slippers sink, sodden in mud. This feels good, the cold earth reaching up to my ankles, anchoring me to the oozing of the living. The coming night croons the promise of heavy rain, the air twanging with a moist feel. The clouds hang bruised and brooding, rumbling throaty and low. Life ripples and rants around me. It is good to be alive, but something is still amiss.

LISTENING

I hear other sounds. Walking away from the street lamp and street, I see movement in the field edging a circle of tall, stretching trees. There are people around a fire, shifting. Sounds of laughter mingle with drumbeats. The drums surge with hollow, rhythmic thuds. Craning my body, I can't see much. Hesitating, the night grows defiant, the clouds bulbous and straining for rain. I should stay in the car. But the drumming lures me, enticing and seductive. My mind races as I slosh through the mud. Nearing the crowd, I see they are dark and dirty, mud-streaked. There are many of them, men and women with teeth flashing and arms jerking. Stunned, I realize they are all bare-chested, feverishly dancing by a large fire. I move to run, but I am rooted, mesmerized. The alluring fire casts shadows on their carousing bodies. Some are humming with the drumbeats. Their hum sweeps across the grass and hovers around me. It strums against my skin, lapping my face, gliding down my neck and melts into my cleavage. The humming pours down my navel and warms the cradle of my belly, bathing me in heat. Their bodies shine with a sticky, twilight sheen. They turn and see me. They beckon me to come closer and join them. Come. Dance. But, I am too fine to wallow in their uncouth, above their guttural romp. I am clean and they are grimed with the earth. They call on me again. I grow rigid and chill myself against the offering of their groveling, beastly prance.

WAKING

I stand aloof, unafraid and unmoving. Their eyes grow cool and scrape me over. Men circle me as others look on. Burly, bawdy and leering, they test me. The men crudely tongue and thrust at my direction, trying to break through my chill and shunning. I hear a woman behind me cackle. One of the men swoops in close, low and bobbing in front of me, shaking crudely. From behind, someone stands close and hisses into my ear, gloating. I flinch. They swarm around me, their wall of sultry rubbing bodies excites me but my eyes hold steely. A woman breaks through the crowd and she bounds up to me, her hips banging side to side, swiveling fast and urgent. She roughly pushes my shoulders, goading me to move. I do not move. She steps away, sneering and pitying my deadness. The drumbeats quicken, the fire flares giant tongues of flame. The fumes blast my flushed face.

I look down; a savage on his knees pinches my thighs. He taunts and jeers. I step back, jumping at his touch. In a rage, I come alive and lunge for them, hurling myself and falling on a hard chest. The reek of their oily, rancid stench smears on me as they shove me back. Stumbling, I fall. Looking down at my arms, I am slathered with their sweat.

Lifting my eyes, seeing the shoving and the grunting, I balk with fear for just a moment. Inhaling the earth's loamy smell, my body snaps open, ready to wrangle and rail. I scramble up. Snarling, Lashing Bitch goes to thunder. She goes to fist, but stops midair, confused. The face in front of me is open and smiling. In circling arms, they weave around me, cheering...for I have...woken. I lower my arms; arms that have been cold and empty for so long.

My rage drains away. Thawing, I choke with wonder. Three women draw me in, pressing breasts and bellies into me, feeding me their heat lovingly, gently. Curled in their womanly bosoms, I begin to jut and twist. I plod. They caress me, dance with me, laughing at my ungainly and awkward shuffling. The graceful, lyrical Giselle has left. I lay exposed. I meet somebody new, Real Bitch.

DANCING

Nudging me with their hips, I yield to their heady rhythm, I find my move. My thighs woo open and my hips roll and undulate as I crouch low to the ground moving languorously. Rising, I whirl around faster and faster, whipping my hair. Spinning and waving my arms, I laugh. I pitch to the right and pitch to the left. A woman leaps up and jacks into the air. I leap up, coil and jack into the air. We pump arms and pound our chests. Thrusting and drenched in the steam of hot bodies, greased with soot, the raw tempo riles me wild and swinging. A hot, sinewy arm snakes around my waist; it's a hard, unrelenting hold. I look up at dark eyes, I could see the flames in his eyes, wickedly glazed and wanting. His body bends forward, spooning me backward. He coaxes me deeper in the curve of him. My thighs fuse into his sweltering skin as his hands scathe the low of my back. I am hungry for his rough, brash groping. I burn for him and his eyes know. I grind into him as I clench my teeth. Our limbs lift and wind around each other as we bristle to the roaring beat. I want to burst over him hard and fast, I want to dance on him. Enflamed, he tantalizes me. He grasps my hair and pulls back my head. He licks my neck and bites my shoulder. We near the fire as we twine, tussle and rub, acrid smoke swirling around our legs. He presses his face to my heaving chest and guzzles in Scorching Bitch. His plunder leaves me trembling and sweetly giddy.

FINDING

Above us, the wind whines and wheezes through the ghostly silhouettes of the tall treetops, branches slapping and thrashing at each other. The sky splits open, bellowing out slashing rain. We push our faces to the sky; our mouths open to tempestuous rain and forest, drinking deeply. The fire fizzles and whimpers down in the crushing sheets of rain, but we scream and laugh, brazen in the heat of our wild searing dance. We fall onto the ground, washed and joyful. Our breaths push out loud as we pant, spent but ferociously alive. Our voracious hearts hammer as fiercely as our grinding. The fever breaks and we quiet down. The rain eases into an easy teasing drizzle. The hue and glint of morning begins to break. Most walk away. No one speaks. I face him, tentative and docile. We are stripped of blazing fire and rampaging dance. I look for softness. I wait. His arms open and gather me. He crushes me into the curve of his soul. Our foreheads touch. Our glistening thighs meet, warm and heavy. A tender sway seeps into our hips and we move together, slowly and sated. The watery light of a new day floats down around us; its shimmer circles us, as we keep ... dancing.

The Car

By J.W. Harkin

While we waited for the stoplight to change, a line of antique cars paraded by; Model T Fords, a 1939 Packard convertible, a 1936 Buick Century sedan with gleaming white sidewalls, and bringing up the rear was a boxy black 1930 Chevrolet two-door coach. I remember that it was called a cast-iron wonder. Its chrome headlamps jutted out from the top of the front fenders like half cantaloupes. It had wide running boards and a spare tire mounted on the back.

My son, who was driving, turned and said, "I'll bet that's an expensive hobby."

I replied, "I was half owner of a 1930 Chevrolet once, but it sure wasn't in as good shape as that one."

"Did you learn a lot, fixing it up?"

"Not much about car mechanics, but I learned something about human nature."

My folks trusted me to drive our 1938 Pontiac from the time I got my driver's license, when I was fifteen. Friends, wanting to double date on Friday or Saturday night, would start calling 30 minutes before I got home from my part-time job. "Could you drive?" they'd ask. I'd tell them that Kurt and I had already made plans. Kurt and I'd been classmates since seventh grade and, although we lived about a mile apart, we were constant companions. Now, we were juniors in high school and best buddies.

One day, almost pulling me along in his excitement, Kurt led me to it, parked forlornly in a vacant lot surrounded by high weeds. "Isn't it beautiful?" His eyes begged me to agree.

"How'd you find it?" I asked, wondering what color it really was under all the oxidized paint. I tried, unsuccessfully, to force open the passenger side door. "It sure needs work."

The 17-year-old 1930 Chevrolet wasn't in bad shape if you discounted the rust, the missing back seat, and the frozen brakes. The engine wouldn't start either. What a piece of junk, I thought.

My face must have shown what I was thinking because Kurt quickly said, "My dad will show us how to repair it. He owned a '30 Chevy. They'll sell it for only $100."

Kurt wanted me to go into partnership with him.

"My dad will even register it in his name," he offered as a clincher to his sales pitch. This surprised me, because his dad was a no nonsense, no frills German, and stingier with a dollar than a Scot.

"If we each put in $75 there'll be enough left over to buy a new battery and the things we need to repair the car."

"How do we share it?" I asked.

Kurt thought for a bit, "We could each get it for a week. Say from Sunday noon to Sunday noon. And it'll have to have a full tank of gas when it gets turned over," he added.

The more I thought about it the better I liked the idea. My Parents' '38 Pontiac needed work that we couldn't afford, and I was interested in learning more about cars by working with Kurt and his dad.

My parents liked Kurt, so once I told them that Kurt's dad would register the car in his name, they gave me their okay. I withdrew $75 from my personal college savings fund.

When the other members of our group learned that Kurt and I had bought a car, some, like Bucky Harrington, who never had a family car to use, said, "Kurt, I wish you'd asked me. It would be great fun to repair."

The next Saturday I saw Kurt's dad towing the old Chevy with Kurt at the wheel. I wondered what had happened, why didn't they include me? Kurt had promised to call when they picked up the car, and whenever they worked on it.

When I asked Kurt, he said, "My dad decided to get the car on the spur of the moment. So we just went ahead and did it. I didn't think you'd mind."

"When are you going to start working on it?" I asked.

"Not today, but I'll call you when we do."

On Sunday afternoon, I went over to Kurt's just to see the car. As I entered their alley, I stopped. The car was up on blocks. The spoke-rimmed wheels were stacked in a pile. Rust-frozen parts soaked in a pail of gasoline. Kurt and his dad wore old working clothes. Their arms were greasy up to their elbows and there were black smudges on their faces where they had wiped away perspiration or shooed a fly.

As I walked into their backyard, I wondered what they would say about not calling me. Kurt's dad smiled and waved when he saw me. They both smelled of gasoline and grease.

Kurt said, "Dad told me that there were more 1930 Chevys built than 1930 Fords and the engine in this is called a 'Stove Bolt Six' because it has six cylinders in line. He says it's also called a 'cast iron wonder'."

What was happening? I had known Kurt for a long time. Why didn't he call me like he had promised? I wanted to learn about cars. I wanted to get my hands greasy too. Unable to speak, I just nodded my head.

Using gasoline, they scrubbed at the grease on their hands and arms. They were done for the day. It was almost time for Sunday dinner.

After his dad went into the house, Kurt continued scrubbing his arms. "We're redoing the entire brake system," he said. "Did you know that it works just like the brakes on a racing bike? You push on the brake pedal and the cables pull the shoes against the brake drums to stop the car. We've inspected the brake cables. We'll have to replace them."

His dad was going to buy some brake shoe material and show him how to cut and rivet it to the metal shoes. They hadn't started on the engine yet, but Kurt said that that shouldn't be a big job. He also said that he was going to build a bench in the back to sit on.

He didn't say anything about why he didn't call; I didn't ask. Bewildered, shoulders hunched, hands deep in my pockets, I walked home, absent-mindedly kicking a tin can that had been in my way.

I never did help repair the Chevy. Kurt never called.

Our family's '38 Pontiac died. We either were going to have a huge repair bill or needed to buy another car, neither of which we could afford. Luckily, my mother took the streetcar to work, and my dad was a trucker and away from home most of the time.

When I got home from my part-time job, the phone didn't ring anymore.

When the Chevy was finally repaired, I asked Kurt about double dating the next weekend. He said, "I'd rather not. I've got this special girl and we'd like to be alone."

When I saw the old Chevy rolling down the street, Lloyd Phillips, the class intellectual, and some girl were sitting on the built-in bench in back. Kurt and his special girl were not alone.

Now that the car was running, it was time to exercise the agreement to take turns. When I asked Kurt, he said, "We're going on vacation for a week, and you can have the car at your house, but my dad doesn't want you to drive it. I guess he's worried about insurance or something." At this, I must have looked shocked because Kurt just shrugged his shoulders and walked off.

The car sat in my backyard all week, a constant reminder that, although I was good enough to help pay for it, I wasn't a good enough risk to drive it. I'd been driving since I was 15. I'd been working part-time after school since I was 14. I was a good student. I wondered if anyone was a good enough risk.

When Kurt and his family returned from vacation, he picked up the old Chevy for his week. Double dating was out; he and Lloyd Phillips had already made plans.

The rebuff by Kurt, coming so soon after the humiliation of not being allowed to drive a car that I owned part of, hurt so much that I thought being stabbed with a knife would feel better.

Bucky Harrington, who was always looking for a ride, reminded me of his interest in the car. Angry and humiliated at the way I had been used, I sold him my share for $75.

When I told Kurt, his face reddened with shock and disbelief. "Why didn't you ask me first?" he yelled.

I yelled back, "I didn't think you'd mind," shrugged my shoulders and walked away.

His dad was angry, when he heard about it.

I thought to myself, what did they expect me to do with half ownership in a car they obviously did not trust me to drive?

Bucky didn't seem to care if Kurt's dad didn't want him to drive the car. He drove it so much and was having so much fun that he would keep driving beyond his allotted time. It became sort of a joke on Kurt, because I knew when he called on Sunday afternoon looking for Bucky, that it might take him until Tuesday to finally corner him and get the car back, and by then it would have an empty gas tank.

After the old Chevy came into our lives, the special relationship with Kurt changed. It was reduced to a nodding in the halls and an acceptance as just another member of our group. Maybe the special relationship only existed in my mind.

As children and teenagers, we too easily put a special trust in people. If this trust is broken, we hurt deeply. I guess we grow up a little too, and begin to build protective barriers of cynicism so that we won't be hurt so much again.

Disconnected

By Melanie Florence

When they told me he was dying,
I knew I shouldn't be bothered
Because I'd been disconnected.

But I went to see him anyway.

A once pompous man,
He had shrunken down
To flashing eyes and gnashing teeth,
Tie-downs, tubes and IVs.
He couldn't talk; he couldn't breathe.

Out of pity,
I gently kissed his brow
And told him I loved him.
He mouthed back, "I love you, too."

Was he speaking the truth?
Or was he twisting me around
To do his bidding?
Either way, I mustn't care
Because I'd been disconnected.

When I saw him again,
Near the end,
He begged me to take him home.
But how could I?
I'd lost the power to help him
When I was disconnected.

That night I dreamed
About him dying alone,

Imprisoned and suffocating
Under anger, resentment, hate
And the failure to appreciate.

Years ago, he told me to leave,
And it was then that I grieved.
When he drove me away,
And fought against my need to stay,
He had played his hand
For it to turn out this way.

Because I'd been disconnected.

Emerald Vision

By Mary Gannon

The week I brought my father, Michael Gannon, back to Ireland after a three decades absence was the anniversary of the 1916 Easter Rising. His brother was dying of colon cancer and there would be no grand reunion or celebrations. Death had spurred this trip. For my father and I the anxious discomfort of takeoff intimated the anxiety of death.

The forces pulled at our hair and skin, a pervasive sense of unease and the unknown. A compressed sensation, mortality, accompanied the pulsing of flesh. As the airplane taxied, I became aware of legs, arms, neck, a sensation of fragility. An elongated perception, vibrations slid through the aircraft.

Moments from earth, the forces pulled me back; the speed intensified. Below the airplane was another kind of security of purpose and event. My breath erupted in fits and starts. The city appeared minor, a scale model of intention as the buildings shrunk until they were barely visible. The continuing hum from the engine and the ascent through the clouds; what was once below was now gone. Feeling torn away from earth, I perceived that our consciousness was finally unneeded. The earth now well below us contained accidents of association, our home, our work. In this ascent to the clouds we experienced the knowledge of how the earth could go on without us.

My father watched as the sun arose in benediction over the horizon. We were about to enter a theme park entitled, "Your history." The Ireland that I knew as his daughter was shaped by oral recitation of family history. And recollection was the great shape shifter fashioning reality into a compromise between event and perception. As the plane descended, the green rolling hills competed with the majestic ocean and a busy urban landscape. These elements repeated the question, where was the real Ireland?

My father's brothers, three of them, waited in the crowded, putty-colored arrival room: shabby and unfinished. It was the waiting room of a country where expansion outpaced its ability to prepare for the onslaught. His terminally ill brother held a sign bearing our family name, Gannon.

These men still dressed like their role models: movie stars of the 30s and 40s adorned in elegant sports coats and double-breasted suits. These were the Gannon Brothers who swaggered through the streets of Dublin; they will not go gentle into being drab, and gray and sloppy. Pensioners, they stood stiff and straight with pride as if the long dead religious Brothers of St. Laurence O'Toole might at any moment inspect collars and cuffs.

When we ventured into the thick traffic of Dublin, we spoke as if time had not passed. They drove my father, Michael, to see the house where he grew up. The family abandoned the dwelling decades before; strangers now inhabited the world of their childhood. This cottage sits in the shadows of multinational corporations exerting global influence. Situated within walking distance of the River Liffey and the emerging international financial services center, the dwelling bore witness to the country's rural beginnings. It seemed as if a handful of cottages were preserved like keepsakes pressed in a diary.

The country has 'moved on' as people like to say at the end of relationships. Ireland embraced the prosperity of a united Europe and the artistic renaissance spawning *The Commitments*, *Riverdance* and the global influence of U2.

Where was the real Ireland? Is that emerald vision contained in memory or in the Celtic Tiger roaring all around us?

Later in that week I hungered for the source of recollection. As I walked about in Merino a neighborhood close to downtown Dublin where my late mother, Eileen, was raised, I searched for the basement where a woman housed her twenty-two children. My mother pondered their fates, their poverty and hunger, throughout her entire life. These images followed her to America. She spoke of them often as if we might walk down our block in Chicago and see their faces pressed against the window.

I studied today's prosperous houses of this Dublin neighborhood where Alfa Romeos and other late model cars parked along the streets. The impoverished Ireland of my mother's childhood was now confined to history books and enshrined in my vivid memories of her stories.

Nostalgia led me to Kilmainham Gaol, the infamous Irish prison built in 1796. The docent tour began with a short film. Contemporary Irish school children announced the names, ages and sentences handed down to boys and girls incarcerated for offenses such as, 'stealing a loaf of bread.' A Celtic *Les Miserables* played out within these load-bearing walls. The tour existed as a medieval nightmare of dank cells with gray stone and prison bars set high on a single wall exposing the anguish of centuries.

The tour guide, an articulate spokesperson for the New Ireland, recounted stories from the 1916 Revolution and how fifteen of its leaders were brought to this jail. These Revolutionaries, sentenced for execution, were shot in the adjoining courtyard. The guide reinforced this injustice by reciting from their last letters. One of them described the romantic and tragic last-minute wedding between Joseph Plunkett and his artist fiancé, Grace Gifford.

The other tourists were unfamiliar with these personal memories, but I knew them well. My maternal grandfather, Robert Humphreys, was a soldier in the Irish Citizen's Army. He fought at St. Stephens Green and at the College of Surgeons in the Easter Rebellion of 1916. Yeats captured this epoch saying, 'a terrible beauty is born.' Their leader, James Connolly, was wounded. After the British surge, Connolly was transported to Kilmainham Gaol. Soldiers carried him on a stretcher to the courtyard where he was tied to a chair and shot.

That act incensed the Irish public and became a resonant symbol of injustice, a nation in agony tied to a chair and shot. My mother repeated that story during my childhood as if that narrative held the key to an ever present reality.

My grandfather lived beyond the Rebellion. When the uprising ended he was arrested and incarcerated for two years at Frongnoch Prison in Wales. During the newly liberated Ireland of the 1920s, he became an insurance agent and soon succumbed to stomach cancer, a direct result, I was told, of the prison's insecticide tainted waters.

My mother relayed the details of the brutal deaths of the 1916 Leaders a thousand times. Vivid images such as the martyrdom of James Connolly were some of the first information presented in my childhood, along with snapshots of a war torn country rife with injustice.

A concord existed between the slain and their surviving generations. History suggests that which is ransomed in one generation will be paid for in another. 'While you smuggled the jewels out as the program commenced, you'll find at the next port of call, a fence will cheat you.'

I recall hearing these 1916 stories as a young child. The bucket of insecticide tainted water sitting in my grandfather's POW camp like a witch hiding in a corner from a fairy tale. Both became the indefinable reality of something that I would come to call "evil." As a child I meditated upon the way in which Tolstoy's unhappy family lamented. 'We were unhappy in our own way.'

Going back to Ireland made me wonder: what were memory and story telling and the carrying of events from place to place but the act of paralyzing time.

A granddaughter who never met her grandfather traced the bullet holes on the College of Surgeons' stately facade. She enacted a wary night's visit that might invoke Hamlet's ghost, but instead she summoned a lone Romanian panhandler. In the twilight of recollection, I have passed that Emerald Vision on to the wind.

15¢ Worth of Soup Greens
A Remembrance

By Carol Sheehan Woolfson

I was peeling an orange the other evening for a fruit salad and was about to put the peels in the garbage disposal when I remembered my childhood when nothing went to waste. The orange peels were put into the prunes stewing on the stove. I was born during The Depression years and though my father never lost his job as an accountant for an insurance company, and I never witnessed a soup line, I know we were beyond careful with money.

Sunday dinners with a roast of some kind (with the leftovers on Monday), which our grandfather - Poppop - carved with a flourish as he stood at the head of the dining room table. This was also the day we got clean linen napkins in our napkin rings to last till the following Sunday. During the month, till Daddy's next paycheck, the roast went from beef, to chicken, to meatloaf - all carved with the same flourish. We ate well.

On Fridays, Mother baked an apple pie from which she always saved some crust to roll up with cinnamon and sugar and baked for my sister, Beps, and me. Or her famous one-egg chocolate cake, or at the very least cookies. Friday was also marketing day and I remember leaning against my mother (she was only 5' tall), as she bargained with the butcher for a good price. Then came one of our best meals - vegetable soup! Shopping for 15c worth of soup greens. Mother had been given a soup bone from the exhausted butcher and then the grocer gave her a small paper bag to put her 15c worth of soup greens into: a potato, a carrot, a small turnip and rutabaga, a handful of green beans, an onion and finally the outer leaf from a cabbage that had seen better days. Believe me we ate all our food because the "starving children in China were always in our minds waiting to give their eyeteeth for a dish like this."

Well, something worked because my sister and I are still around. Was it the 15c worth of soup greens or the spoonful of "Hep-Iron" that we took every day...or the love that we always felt?

Enjoy! Carol.

"Commies. You're studying to be commie," whispered Bruce.

"Young lady?" Mrs. Sommers' voice rang loudly. "Do you have something to share with the class?"

Gina stared at her desk.

I stood up. "Our friend Denise Ann Makowsky is having important visitors from another country." I waited for permission to go on.

"Go on," said Mrs. Sommers.

"We'll be like ambassadors, ambassadors of the United States. Like Secretary General U Thant at the United Nations. Remember our class trip? He said it's everyone's job to be friendly to people of the world. Help them understand democracy and stuff."

Bruce laughed out loud. Why didn't the teacher hear him say "*Ewww* Thant?"

Gina jumped in to save me. "They're coming from Albania and we want to make them feel welcome so we've having a party."

"Gina, did I hear you're researching the country?" Mrs. Sommers took off her glasses to wipe a spot. "You might try the National Geographic to learn more."

"And Gina, Eva," she continued. "You are to write a composition about what you learn from this experience and share it with the class."

Out of the corner of my eye I could see Bruce Dreyfus smiling. I hated his sniveling face.

He said in a low, whiney voice. "*Ewww* Thant is gonna call the FBI and put you and your fat Grandma in jail for being commie sympathizers."

"For extra credit, of course," Mrs. Sommers said as she turned back to the blackboard. "Something you can use, both of you."

I thrust my fist in the direction of Bruce's jaw. I didn't mean to punch him but his face got in the way. My hand hurt but it felt really good. I didn't even mind staying in after school that afternoon.

Hail, Albania

By Brenda Dareff Kuhlman

Growing up in the shadow of the United Nations made us kids feel worldly and sophisticated. Okay, maybe we lived a subway ride away; but the U.N. was our class trip in 5th grade. During the tour, we got the Secretary General to wave at us. His name was U Thant, which I thought was pretty neat.

"It rhymes with *who*," I told Grandma Berta. I stood with my back to her as she measured around my shoulders for a sweater she'd been knitting. It wasn't for me, though. She mailed everything she knitted: bulky sweaters, granny square blankets, and wool caps to her sister's family in Hungary.

"Are you done?" I asked.

She nodded, straight pins held tightly in the corner of her mouth. I scooted out the fire escape to my friend Jill's apartment on the third floor.

I rapped on the window. Denise opened the latch and I climbed into their small kitchen. I could smell remains of a boiled chicken supper.

Denise was holding a dishtowel. When she saw me, she waved it like a flag.

"Guess what, Eva?"

"You got tickets to see the Beatles at Shea Stadium?" I was crazy about the new band from England.

"I wish," she sighed. "No. But we're getting company."

Another rap sounded on the window. It was Gina, our best friend from the first floor. She climbed in and we turned silent for a moment. We touched pinkies, our secret Girls' Club handshake.

"So, who's coming?" I asked.

"Company. Friends of my mother." Denise picked up a casserole dish and began wiping. "They have a girl who is eleven and a boy, too. I think he's eight."

"Maybe we'll have enough people for a kickball team," Gina said. She was the athletic one, always trying to organize a game.

"Dunno," Denise looked downward, concentrating on her drying. "They may not know what kickball is."

"Where are they from, like Mars?" Gina said.

"Well, they're not from around here."

Gina raised an eyebrow. "From another country?"

"Um, they knew my dad from the camps."

The tiny kitchen grew quiet for the second time. Denise wasn't talking about sleep-away camps in the Catskills. When her father wore short sleeves, we could see blue numbers on his arm. He'd been at Bergen-Belsen, a place we'd heard plenty about when grownups thought we weren't listening.

"Well," Gina brightened. "We'll have to make them feel welcome. Like throw a party."

"I'll make a cake, a chocolate cake," I said. After my Suzy Homemaker Oven overheated, Grandma let me use her oven.

"We can learn about their country," Gina continued. "Customs, the culture, holidays. Just like in Mrs. Sommers' class."

"Maybe we can get extra credit!" I announced.

Denise giggled. "Extra credit's not gonna help you at this point."

I ignored her. "So where in Europe are they from?"

"France? We could sing the Bastille Day song," said Gina.

"Italy? Gina's mom could make meatballs," I said. "Or maybe Portugal? Brazil? Grandma Berta said lots of Jews went there after the war."

Denise considered this for a moment. "No, I think it starts with an A."

We went through the alphabet. Africa? Alsace Lorraine? Asia Minor?

Denise went to look for her father's National Geographic. She returned and thumbed through pages as we looked over her shoulder.

"Algeria?" Gina read aloud. "Angola? Antigua? Armenia?"

Denise frowned. "It's something like Armenia."

"Albania?"

"Yes!"

The next day at school, I skipped recess and spent time in the school library, flipping pages of the A-B volume of Compton's Encyclopedia. Albania, it turned out, was anoth[er] country in that part of the world with a history of be[ing] invaded. A lot. Most recently it was Mussolini. That [made] out meatballs. I returned to the book but skipped ahe[ad to] other interesting things. There was a gross picture o[f] and really ugly alligators. I considered memoriz[ing the] encyclopedia, starting with A. Maybe it would e[xcuse me] from going to school. I pondered this until the be[ll for] the next period.

Back in class, Gina sat behind me and [Bruce] Dreyfus sat beside me, as usual.

"You'd think teachers would have a be[tter way of] seating kids. I've put up with him since ki[ndergarten] he pulled my hair and stole my pencils. Ju[st because] names are in alphabetical order," I told [her while he] making tiny burping noises that only I c[ould hear.]

"I know," Gina whispered. "L[isten. The capital of] Albania is Tirana, and it's on the Adr[iatic. The money] is the *Lek*."

"The lake?"

"No, that's just how your [money   ]
Bruce Dreyfus.

We ignored him. "It's a le[k   ]
main industries are textiles, [   ]
wheat? Something agricultura[l   ]

Gina brought balloons and pink crepe paper left over from her sister's engagement party. She set her poster in front of a large potted plant. It showed a map and listed the major exports of Albania.

My cake looked really professional, the yellow writing contrasting well with the chocolate frosting. I stood back to admire it.

"WE COME TO AMERICA?" asked Gina.

"Oh my God, I forgot the L in WELCOME! What am I going to do?"

"No one will notice," Denise called over from her station at the window. She'd been sucking the empty icing tube.

"Sure they will."

"I have an idea," said Gina. "Use some spaghetti."

"On cake?"

"I mean uncooked spaghetti," Gina said. "Hey, I just thought of something. What if they don't speak English?"

"Don't worry. I asked Mr. Kasem down at the fruit stand. He taught me some words in Albanian."

"They're here!" announced Denise, watching from the fire escape.

In a moment of incredible brilliance, I spotted a toothpick near the cubed Velveeta appetizers. It folded easily for a quick "L," and I was free to join in greeting our new friends.

"Wel-come-to-our-home," Denise shouted, speaking slow enough to emphasize each syllable.

"What are you shouting for?" Denise's mother said sharply. "Nobody's hard of hearing."

Denise apologized and softened her voice. "These are my best friends, Gina and Eva."

We curtsied.

"*Mirc se vjen,*" I said in my new favorite language. It came out sounding like *Messy One* when Mr. Kasem taught it to me.

I continued. "*Gezohen qu te takova.* Pleased to meet you."

The adults looked at me, puzzled. Denise's mother remembered her manners, admonishing the guests to "Sit, sit already."

The girl was still staring at me. She didn't look like the newspaper photographs of girls from Eastern Europe. There were no dark circles under dark, brooding eyes. In fact, her eyes were bright blue. She didn't wear work shoes either but instead black patent leather Mary Janes. I would have killed for a pair of shoes like that.

Drinks were poured: schnapps in crystal glasses for the adults and Hawaiian Punch in Dixie cups for kids. We sat on the plastic covered couch, which was hot and uncomfortable.

Denise's mother looked up from her conversation with the adults. "Girls, girls. Take Linda and Michael outside and go and play."

Linda? I expected her name to be Gretel or Babushka. I would have killed for a pretty name like Linda.

We charged down the stairs. Even Linda seems relieved to be out of the stuffy apartment.

We were all over her with questions.

"Do you go to a state controlled Communist school?" I asked. "Do you have to wear a Communist uniform? Do they tell you religion is bad?"

"Are you allowed to talk to boys?" asked Denise. "Do they let you have a telephone? Do you have a television?"

"What is it like to be a refugee kid? Did they make you get shots? Did you escape in the middle of the night?" Gina had been watching a lot of television lately.

Linda only shrugged.

"Don't you talk? Can you talk English?"

"We'll slow down so you can understand."

Gina raised her hand. "I think it's time for entertainment."

We lined up as we'd practiced and sang what I had found in the library: the Albanian National Anthem.

"For the Lord himself has said that nations vanish from the earth.

But Albania shall live on. It is for her that we fight.
Hail, hail Albania."

There was an awkward silence. That was a good sign. I figured that Linda was getting choked up with emotion and homesickness for her former land.

"For your information," she finally spoke, without a trace of accent. "I know English. And all those questions are N.O.Y.B.: none of your business. And I think that girls in Queens are the weirdest people in the whole world."

Gina saved the day. "We don't care. But do you play kickball?"

We played ball, trying to ignore the insult. After all, children of concentration camp survivors have a hard time. I was at first base (the mailbox) when I slid on the sidewalk trying to tag Gina. The game was called on account of my scraped knee.

I told Grandma Berta about the visiting family while she sprayed my cut with iodine.

"The Ackermans are here?"

I nodded. "Their English is really good. And the kid, Linda? She's just like us."

"Why shouldn't she be just like you?"

"Because of the horrible atrocities committed by her country, that Socialist Republic behind the Iron Curtain," I said.

Grandma put her finger on the top of the Band-Aid to kiss it to good health. Then she put her arms around me.

"So this is what you girls have been so busy with? Learning about Eastern Europe?"

I nodded. "Denise's family knew them from the camps so we wanted to make them feel welcome. They'll like it in the USA. We were welcoming ambassadors, like the Secretary General of the U.N."

"I'm sure you were, dear. I'm sure you were."

I heard a giggle escape from the corner of her mouth where straight pins usually stick out. The giggle turned into a full laugh.

Was she having a fit? Grandma Berta was a no-nonsense woman who didn't laugh much. Like, never. This was weird.

She pulled me close. I could smell the VO-5 in her hair.

"Are you okay, Grandma?"

She took a tissue from where it was tucked in the bottom of her sleeve and dabbed her eyes. Still shaking her head, she said something in Yiddish that I think meant "Such a good girl." She sighed heavily.

"Yes, dear. The Ackermans did come from Eastern Europe. Poland, not too far from where me and Grandpa lived." She closed her eyes. "Your Grandpa, may he rest in peace, knew Denise's papa in the camps."

"But the Ackermans? They came after the war," she continued. "Nineteen hundred and forty-five or forty-six is when. And the Ackermans, they didn't stay in the city. They were farmers. They moved upstate. To Albany."

"Albany?"

"Albany. Not Albania."

"Albany in New York?" My voice screeched. "Oh God, we made such fools of ourselves."

"Nonsense," Grandma smiled. "It was a grand thing that you did, and I am very, very proud..."

"What will Mrs. Sommers say?" I was mortified.

"Well, I'd be happy to tell her I've never seen such effort put in a welcoming of new people," she said. "You and your friends, you're a regular United Nations. The Secretary General: what was his name? U Thant? He'd be very pleased."

"Really?"

"Just next time. Change the words of the national anthem."

"To what?"

"Hail, Albany."

A Hawk in the Park

By Don Collier

You are enjoying your summer vacation as an eleven-year old: baseball, swimming pool, summer camp, and cookouts. Then one day a little boy drops in to visit your neighbor. Perry is loud, crude and wild, but he is your age, and you get paired with him one evening by arrangement with your parents. The two of you are provided funds for amusements at the Fairgrounds, just a brief walk from your house in western Birmingham, to entertain yourselves while the older folks do something else. There is enough money for tickets to most of the rides and a snack or two.

The night is cool and the weather clear - ideal for a summer evening in the park. The thrill of the park - the bright colored lights; the smell of corn dogs and cotton candy; the shrieks of children being whirled up and around - takes your mind off the dubious qualities of your companion. Going at full speed, you take a fraction of a moment - no more - to exploit the Pony Ride, Boat Ride, snack stands, Swings, Tilt-a-Whirl, Roller Coaster, Bumper Cars and the Ferris Wheel.

Then, out of cash and flush with time and appetite, you stroll around the Fairgrounds looking for something; anything; nothing. The clock comes to a halt. You pass the popcorn, peanut and cotton candy vendors several times; the ticket booths many more times; each of the rides; and hundreds of tourists doing much the same thing. Won't someone come forward - a generous adult or a sympathetic ticket taker - to give you free rides or free food?

Then there it is! A double fistful of ride tickets in the hand of a distracted middle-aged woman with two children in tow! Perry says, "Let's grab those tickets!"

You hesitate.

"Come on!" he says.

You balk again.

"Let's go!" he pleads.

You just stand there.

Perry takes off on his own, grabs the tickets from the lady and speeds off on foot to God knows where. You stay frozen in your tracks. The woman shrieks, then shouts, "Hey, come back here with my tickets!"

She sees you. "Weren't you with that boy who just stole my tickets?"

"No, ma'am."

She pages an attendant while you remain frozen, not knowing where or whether to run. You stick it out. The attendant says, "Who was the boy you were with?"

"I don't know," you lie again. "I just met him a little while ago." After giving them your name and phone number, the authorities let you go, and you go home alone.

Not knowing in advance that Perry would get his just rewards the next day, you lie in bed that night, not able to sleep; re-living every word spoken by Perry, the woman and the attendant; re-viewing and critiquing and amending where necessary every action you took; and hearing the haunting echoes off your lies. You ask your mother, "Is there something you can take to make you forget?"

I Look For Myself Again

By Betty Hyland

I looked for myself today at International airport. While I watched for my friend to come through the Customs door, I searched the faces of the other passengers to see if I was among them—or rather if the person identical to me was.

I know she exists. My Uncle Joe once told me. I was eight years old and we were sitting on the back porch of his farmhouse one summer afternoon husking corn. Flies buzzed in the flypaper hanging from the ceiling. Sauerkraut foamed in a crock behind us.

"The law of averages dictates that everyone has a double," he said that day, slapping his big rough hands together in emphasis. He had been reading a scientific journal. He owned a general store in town and had time to kill between customers so he liked having reading material around, especially maps, almanacs and those scientific journals.

"Could I have a double?" I wondered, pulling corn silk off my braids.

"I'll bet you could, Betty Ann. Somewhere—I don't know where—maybe Australia or France or up near the North Pole—there could be a little girl who looks exactly like you."

By this time, I had stopped husking corn and was listening intently. "Is my double's birthday the same as mine?" I asked.

"Maybe she's already nine years old. It seems to me though," he recollected, "the article said that a double wouldn't necessarily have to be alive the same time you are. Maybe your double won't be born until the next century or maybe she lived back in the days of Robin Hood."

He must have seen the disappointment on my face because he quickly added, "but probably she's the exact same age as you."

As often happened with Uncle Joe, he had gotten in over his head.

"Could I be triplets?" I asked.

"I don't think so, but with all the people in China, it's possible there are three identical little Chinese girls somewhere. Maybe one in Shanghai, one in the Gobi Desert, and one way up on the border near Outer Mongolia." He polished a Macintosh apple on his shirtsleeve and took a bite.

I imagined the girls screaming in delight when they met unexpectedly at a Chinese dragon parade dressed in identical silk robes and carrying identical paper kites.

This same reliable law of averages, Uncle Joe went on to tell me, dictated that the chance was one in many millions that you would ever meet your double, but it was certain everybody had one. "There's just so many ways of arranging noses and chins and knees and things," he explained, unscientifically.

It all made sense to me, especially since it was backed up by that article.

"I'll bet my double's name is Audrey," I told him, for no reason I can remember now. I was staring across the cow pasture toward a distant land at a little girl who looked exactly like me. I wondered what her parents looked like and whether she had a sister like mine. Did she have an Uncle Joe? What language did she speak? Was she left-handed and did she have the same brown freckle by her right eye?

I used to be on the lookout for her from time to time throughout my early years. There was always the chance she lived close by and I didn't want to miss her. I'd search the faces of people passing in trains and buses.

I have a particular memory of imagining we had chanced upon each other in an ice cream parlor. We laughed and talked for hours about how astonishingly alike we were. We even had both ordered double-scoop, vanilla/chocolate ice cream cones.

Still I never found Audrey. I don't know what distant memory made me look for her today at the airport. She wasn't there. But she's somewhere—a little thinner, maybe. A little blonder.

I know she exists because my Uncle Joe didn't lie.

Probably she took an earlier flight.

In a Moment of Selfish Silence

By Kennedy Kelly

They had talked about it over dinner, in voices both worried and hopeful.

"Just until we get on our feet," my mother said.

My parents needed the money desperately, and so, Kay, who had been a secretary during the War, was going back to work. It was the late 1940s when it wasn't considered right for a woman to leave her child with strangers. Still, it was humiliating to keep taking handouts from family, in order to put food on the table. And so I, the cause of the too-stretched paycheck and my mother's crying—and maybe the benders that soothed my father from time to time—was going to day care.

That first day, we were late. At four years old, I remember being pulled along.

"Would you hurry," my mother yelled over her shoulder. A bit roughly led, almost yanked, I tried moving my short, scrawny legs faster. Suddenly, my mother stopped, gathered herself and took a deep breath. Squarely in front of us stood the biggest house I had ever seen. I tipped my head back as far as it would go, looking up the wide concrete steps, past the huge front doors, and higher and higher, as the brownstone's massive red bricks reached clear up to the sky, making me feel a little dizzy. My mother took no notice of the house or of me. She had been there before, of course, to make the arrangements for my day care. Today, she was more concerned about the impression that we were making than the terror silently spreading through her young daughter. Hurrying now off to work, she deposited me quickly inside the dark, strange place with its scuffed walls and the other discarded children.

If my mother had misgivings about leaving me, they didn't show. As she walked back out the door, there might have been the faintest scent of freedom regained, a lightness in her step, having shed at least temporarily the thing that kept her poor, and sometimes even hungry.

I don't recall much about day care, but I do remember in great detail nap time every afternoon. Bunk beds, set close together in a narrow room, seemed to be stacked up to the ceiling. I worried that they would make me sleep on the top bunk, but it turned out that those precarious perches were assigned to the older kids. The new kids, like me, stayed on the bottom, where we couldn't fall out and hurt ourselves. None of the other children seemed to have any problem sleeping on command, and every afternoon they curled into blissful slumbering shapes almost instantly. Crying silently, thumb in mouth and lying very still, I couldn't fall asleep. I couldn't even close my eyes. What if my parents came while I was sleeping? Would they decide to leave me overnight? Or forever?

Without warning those fears came to an end. Driving home one night, from the back seat of the car, I was surprised to hear my mother tell my father that she wasn't going to bring me back to day care any more.

"They say that she cries all day. I can't bear to think about her being so unhappy, Bill. We're just going to have to find another way to do without," she said in a firm but worried voice to my father.

Secretly, her decision made me feel very happy. Not because I hated day care – the truth was that after two weeks I started to make friends. But the decision had been made.

More importantly, what I saw clearly—even at that tender age—was that my parents were choosing my happiness over theirs. Such a selfless expression of their love for me rarely happened in our harsh existence, and I greedily relished that feeling. What I didn't fully realize until much later was the price we would all pay for a moment of selfish silence.

My sin of omission began a chain of events that spiraled downward for years. We never had enough money, and the walls of our world seemed to close in on us.

Hopelessness strangled my mother into an unyielding gloom. My father coped in the traditional Irish way, and hid from his pain, inside the bottle.

And how did I -- unconsciously believing myself to be the cause of all this -- cope? At first, childish comforts sufficed, then escalated—thumb sucking, hair chewing, nails bitten to the bloody quick. Still a vague guilt, that I did not understand, sat on my heart and haunted me silently well into my adult years.

Eventually, mercifully, through the resilience of the human spirit and the healing of time, a blessed clarity evolved, and with it, absolution. I came to realize that my parents had been predestined for depression and alcoholism by their own damaged childhoods. I was not responsible for their scars. Regardless of whether that little girl had spoken up that fateful day in the car, our lives might have turned out exactly the same.

A Lifetime of Vacations, All in One Day

By John C. Stipa

Have you ever been out driving and noticed one sneaker, and just one, lying in the middle of the road? Did you ask yourself: "I wonder who that sneaker belonged to?" And I'll bet you that question was followed by: "Where is the other one?" Well, keep reading, because I know the owner of those sneakers, personally.

Prior to 1980, Atlantic City thrived as the dominant ocean resort of New Jersey. Expansive beaches, attractions unlike any other and an endless boardwalk drew tourists by the thousands. Unfortunately, the city fell into decline causing New Jersey to look for an infusion of economic stimulation. More likely east coast developers with big egos were tired of Las Vegas having all the fun. Not surprisingly, real estate became "an opportunity" that Donald Trump and the Casinos (sounds like a rock 'n' roll band from the 50s) capitalized on. The Donald invaded the town and converted it to a place where high rollers could look forward to years of fun that didn't require a plane ticket to Nevada. But I remember when a lifetime of vacations could be had in one day. And you didn't need a plane.

At five AM on summer Sunday mornings, my father began preparations for the family excursion to Atlantic City. Three-dozen beach buckets, seven towels, four chairs, three umbrellas and one magic blanket tied to the top of a beat-up Chevrolet station wagon. To say everything was "tied to the top" is not fair, to my father, anyway. The man could do amazing feats with a thousand feet of clothesline. If you envision the Grinch's sleigh and mountains of belongings lashed to the roof, the picture becomes clearer.

With the hotel-on-wheels ready for departure, my sisters and I were transported, via my mother's caring arms, from snuggly havens of slumber to the cold, unforgiving metal floor of a bed created by folding down the back seat. No seatbelts, no airbags, no car seats. If we were lucky, we got a blanket to lay on top of the hinges that dug into our ribs. And we loved it. As far as my three sisters and I were concerned, we were riding in a chariot to adventure.

Pillows?

"Not necessary," my dad pontificated - provoking a tidal wave of childhood woe - how he slept on straw before his family could afford a mattress or on broken glass during WWII. So we improvised and slept in the shape of a square, using one person's rear end as a pillow while offering our own to a sibling. The arrangement worked well except my sisters claimed my feet stank worse than rotten clams and demanded I stick them out the window. Like any typical ten-year-old boy, I took my sisters' input under serious advisement and ignored them. Now you know how I lost the first of my sneakers.

Most normal people took the AC Expressway to Atlantic City. Both major bridges out of Philadelphia, the Walt Whitman and the Ben Franklin, connected with New Jersey's super highway to the resorts.

"Not scenic enough," my Dad proclaimed, launching into a dissertation on the benefits of crossing the Tacony Palmyra bridge (only 35 cents) onto old Route 73. I guess twenty-foot plaster statues of lumberjacks used to promote roadside stores were a rarity in those days.

Even rarer, was my Dad's internal GPS. Before the casinos threw up their boisterous profiles Atlantic City didn't have a skyline causing me to wonder how he possibly knew we were almost there. All I saw were tall reeds and swampland.

"How do you figure?" I said.

Silently, my Dad rolled down the window to let in the smell of barnacles, clams and ocean spray. I slumped back in my seat. The wry smile on his face confirmed what we always knew: the man was clairvoyant. To this day, I relish the thrill of teaching my daughters a lesson by way of wordless theatrics.

When we parked to unload however, silence departed and chatter filled the air as we transferred the day's provisions to our young backs. Eager to dip our toes in the ocean, we charged ahead with the arm-swing of power joggers on steroids. Across the dusty parking lot, through the jagged hole in the chain-link fence and onto the rocky dirt path, we merged with other day-trippers doggedly determined to establish a beachhead. Elbows jostled, provisions were repurposed as defensive mechanisms and a pecking order was established. Between narrow buildings and winding alleys we weaved; an endless column of human pack mules. Panting and sweating, we ignored the heat from molten streets as we gained the sidewalk. Up the steps to a splinter-infested boardwalk, our short-lived exuberance draining with the climbing sun. Down more steps to a stretch of sand with no end in sight.

"Did someone move the ocean?"

"Are we lost?"

"Mom! I'm dizzy."

"Is that a palm tree?"

"No, Anucha," my mother kindly replied to Anna, my sister. "It's an Italian Water Ice stand."

"I want some!" I wailed. Not for my crusty throat, but for my broiling feet.

Soon everyone went to tiptoe as if only a millisecond of contact with the sun-baked sand would somehow alleviate the burning. A few more steps and we glanced at the yawning distance to the sea. Then at each other. Confusion. Then clarity.

"Run!" my Dad yelled.

And we sprinted. A band of gypsies struggling to maintain control of their load. First a bucket fell.

"Let it go," my Dad cheered. "We have more."

Thighs earned their pay as we plowed through the deep sand. A blanket dropped, then a chair. Only one hundred yards to go. Soon, provisions began to fall more quickly. And not by accident.

Like a pack of wild animals, we tossed the last bucket and hurtled across the hardened sand into the icy surf. Arms pin-wheeling, balance failing, bodies surged into the ocean, ending in a drunken collapse under the waves.

At last, coolness tickled my skin. Sweat dissolved. My scalp tingled. A shiver ripped down my spine, goose bumps erupted everywhere. Refreshing and invigorating. Digging our toes into the quicksand, we blasted off the bottom, broaching the surface like frolicking dolphins.

"WAHOO!"

"Yeah baby!"

Other whoops of joy were soon followed by war cries of "Get Daddy!" starting a briny rumble. After my dad cried Uncle, we walked back to the beach and laughed at the breadcrumb trail of beach provisions that stretched to the boardwalk.

We staked our squatting post by setting buckets around the perimeter like sentries. Umbrellas were planted, chairs unfolded, towels draped and sun tan lotion flowed. Finally, the magic blanket unfurled. Somehow, it spanned the entire area. The cooler found a home in the shade and faster than Navy SEALS on covert, we made camp.

No one was allowed to leave the safety zone of the blanket until properly protected by the solar repelling might of Coppertone's fantastic factor 4.

"Don't forget the tops of your feets," Mom said.

I remember all of us looking down in unison at the substantial lathering of white cream. "Feets are good, Mom," my sister Loretta said and we exploded from the campsite, our only plan being to cram everything into a few precious hours.

My older sisters would set off in search of teenage boys. I for sand crabs. My younger sister sat in the shallow surf, drizzling sand into castle towers.

Beneath Million Dollar Pier, I found a dozen other boys my age and learned a lifelong lesson my cell-phone-texting, IM-sending, void-of-interacting kids of today could never understand: how to make short time friends in a face-to-face situation. Our mission: catch as many sand crabs as possible.

"You there," someone would take the Conn. "Dig a pit on dry land. We need a jail." There were no complaints of increased workload and low pay. It was a job that needed to be done. Within seconds, a detention facility emerged. Before the deadline and under budget.

Million Dollar Pier used to extend one thousand feet into the Atlantic Ocean. We couldn't fathom that our task was hopeless. It wasn't physics or lack of ability. We were simply out-numbered. After an hour of intense scooping and transporting the crustacean criminals, we grew frustrated and shifted to an objective only a gang of boys could imagine: hold back the ocean. Instead of digging into the sand, we pushed it en masse to form a wall. It was under the boardwalk that we learned physics. In one wave, the Great Wall of New Jersey was destroyed and with it, our hope. Panting and sweating, we stood, demoralized.

A scream erupted from the surf diverting our attention from the catastrophe. We looked about in frenzied awe.

"Someone's been bitten by a shark!"

A gangly kid pointed a freckled arm. "Look!"

All eyes followed his index finger to the surf as a curvy teenage girl galloped out of the waves in screaming hysteria.

"Get it off! Help! Shark! It's biting me! Ouch! Get it off me!" The girl's hair snarled a Medusa-like mess about her head and something flopped behind her as she ran.

"Look at that idiot girl with all the seaweed in her hair," a boy with a Beatles' haircut said. "That's no shark. It's a crab and it won't let go of her foot. What a loser." All the boys burst into laughter. All except one.

I turned Beatle boy's shoulder and slugged him in the jaw.

Spittle flew from my mouth. "That's my sister, jerk-off," I said in between iron fists. Beatle boy made no move to retaliate. I ran to my sister.

Maria rolled on the sand, clutching her ankle. A crowd gathered. "Johnny, get it off me. Hurry."

Like a triage medic, I focused on the Frisbee-sized crab that had dug its claw into my sister's toe. Fear gripped my spine as I looked into the face of the monster that reminded me of the horror movies on Doc Shock's Creature Double Feature. I glanced at Maria's panic-stricken eyes and learned the meaning of 'sometimes a man's got to do what a man's got to do.'

With my bare hand, I grabbed the crab's claw. The crustacean's other pincher gored my forearm as I ripped Maria free. Swooping in, my mom carried her away to the magic blanket for emergency room treatment of a band-aid and hair smoothing. I stood there, crab in my hand, its other claw still embedded into my arm. Smiling, I plucked the crab off and tossed the remains at Beatle boy. To this day, Maria will not go in the ocean without the protection of water shoes. To this day, when faced with do or die scenarios, the vision of that crab staring me in the face flashes through my brain.

As the crowd dispersed, Dad whisked me away to the knee-deep water of a sandbar fifty yards off shore.

"Best place to find clams, Giovanni," he said and then formed the fingers of each hand into the shape of a knife. Bending over, he drove them into the soft sand, felt around and rose with two clamshells. As I gawked, he smashed them together, flicked away unnecessary pieces of shell, extracted the innards and swallowed them whole.

"Go get your bucket," he said, a mischievous grin on his face. "We're having steamers for dinner."

"GIOVANNI!" Mom yelled from camp. "Time for lunch."

"Come on, Pop, I'll race you." I set off doing a high step through the waves. Chuckling, I told myself there is no way an old man can whup a kid speedster.

In my peripheral vision, I caught sight of a human form gaining on me. I continued to thrash through the wading pool, but soon I humbly slowed to a halt as my dad cruised by, swimming a relaxing free-style. Never challenge a Navy man to a footrace in the ocean.

On the sunny side of Million Dollar Pier, concession stands, rides and arcade booths baited naïve tourists. A beefy red-haired guy in the water tank called out. "Hey kid, betcha can't dunk me."

My mouth opened to answer the challenge. "After lunch, Giovanni," my mom intervened. I pointed a revengeful index finger, the universal symbol of "Gonna get you."

We weaved our way through the maze of attractions to the coolness of the food court canopy. Italian water ice and hoagie "sangwhiches" were always the most popular stations amid the smorgasbord of offerings. My Dad opted for a wax cup of strange morsels of mortadella, peppers, onions, cappicola, cauliflower and onions; better known as antipasto.

"Pop, can I try some?" I asked.

Extending his arm, he offered me a choice.

I plopped some strange looking tongue-like thing with a squishy texture into my mouth. The contorted look of disgust across my face caused my dad to laugh.

"How about a sangwhich, Giovanni?" Quickly he fetched me a six-inch section.

I bit into the Italian roll and nearly broke my teeth trying to penetrate the hard exterior. Determined, I ripped away a chunk and closed my eyes at the wonderful combination of salty prosciutto, spicy pepperoni, salami and the driest provolone cheese that melted in my mouth. I sighed, a contented smile on my face. Oh the simple pleasures.

"*Mangia soppra tutto*, Giovanni," my dad conveyed another life lesson. "Eat above anything else."

Sufficiently fed, my sisters and I burst from the food court to the mercy of the arcade.

"Come toss the ring!" one barker shouted.

"Don't listen to him, kid," the adjoining attendant said. "The basketball foul shot is for you."

Ignoring the piranhas, I beelined it to the dunk tank.

"Ho-Ho!" The red-haired guy scoffed. "So you're back. Come on kid, hit me with your best shot."

Plunking my dollar down, I received three baseballs. Three times the sopping wet dunkee climbed back up the ladder. "You stink kid," he yelled as I walked away after the last perfect strike. I smiled. Never challenge a future Division 1 collegiate baseball pitcher to a dunking contest.

A bigger challenge for my younger sister and me was snaring French fries that my mother held out to us as we flew by in miniature dune buggies. In between munches, we laughed at our misses and blasted away at the horn buzzers that sounded like Jimi Hendrix's guitar in epileptic shock.

Within an hour, our ration of money set aside for rides gone, we returned to the beach.

Tired from the morning's escapades, I plopped my skinny body into a beach chair. The full extent of the magnificent playground of limitless imagination lay before me. To the left, a football game and Frisbee Ultimate; to the right, whiffle ball and soccer; straight ahead, old men tried to squeeze a game of Bocci in between kids digging a fort.

Joggers interrupted my view of the aqua-green ocean. As the shirt-less exerciser disappeared under the pier, I spotted a lonely, scrawny boy flying a kite, then a guy in a Gilligan hat and cut-off jeans, hovering a metal detector just above the sand. Next to him, a sweaty man with huge calves, dressed in all white, lugged half a refrigerator from a shoulder strap. What idiot would want a job selling ice cream under such intense heat? The scream of swimmers drew my attention back to the ocean. Chicken fights and body surfers. Inner tubes and rafts. Europeans in skimpy bikinis; the women's not as skimpy as the men's.

The roar of a speedboat reverberated in my ears. As I followed it against the horizon, wondering when the annoying thrumming would end, I picked up a similar sound and looked skyward. Against a sky made bluer by the pure whiteness of fluffy clouds, a prop plane droned along, pulling a sign advertising a crab dinner special at the Hotel Roma.

"Look Mom, dinner special at that hotel we stayed at last year. Remember, the one where Dad made Anna hide because they charged by the person."

"I remember," Mom said and shifted her gaze to the bandage on Maria's toe. "But I don't think a crab dinner will go over well tonight."

"Right," I said, turning my attention back to the kaleidoscope of umbrellas and bathing suits. I closed my eyes to see if I could recognize something by its sound or smell.

Amid the din of a million people chattering, I picked out the crashing of the waves, so soothing and constant. The therapeutic whoosh never lasted long enough, inevitably interrupted by the elongated whistle of the lifeguard reining in his flock. Then as the welcomed whoosh returned, I picked out Jerry "The Geeter With The Heater" Blavat on radio AM 560 WFIL introducing The Rolling Stones. Mick Jagger in high pitch reminded me of seagulls closing in for a kill. I never understood why those strange animals were so often included in the same sentence as the phrase 'the calming caw of seagulls.' To me, the rats with wings deserved nothing but to have seashells chucked at them.

After chasing away the last of the vultures, I followed the sun as it slid down the western sky and how it changed color from white to red. Amazingly, so did our skin.

The appearance of sunburn was Mom's alarm clock. "Time to go," she announced.

"Aw, Mom. Can't we stay to see the diving clown show? I heard a horse is going to jump into the ocean with them."

"Maybe next time, Anucha. Daddy has to work tomorrow."

The heat of the day gone with the setting sun, we took our time trudging across the vast beach to the boardwalk, savoring every step, burning every memory of the day's events into our brain cells forever.

Arriving at the car, an unattended garden hose provided a poor man's shower. While we cleaned up, my Dad reloaded the Grinch's sleigh. Tired and sunburned, we lay with our feet out the back window. We only stopped once to raid a roadside fruit stand. The back of the car filled with the sweet smell of the peach juice that dribbled down my chin.

"The peach smells better than your feet, Johnny," my sister Anna said before the rhythmic "thwick, thwick, thwick" of the station wagon's tires on old Route 73 lulled her to sleep. In a moment of illumination, it came to me why my dad chose that particular road for the ride home.

Smiling, I tossed my other sneaker out the window and drifted off to the nap of a lifetime.

Little Duke's Funeral

By Diane Hunter

My childhood memories are like turning the pages of a favorite book, yellowed and worn with time, and finding my smile. This is one of those smiles.

Mid-July 1949 in Natrona Heights, Pennsylvania was predictable—hot, steamy and uneventful. I was nine years old and happy to be idling away my day taking refuge in the shade of our front porch and sipping on a frosty grape Nehi.

My older brother, Bob, and his friend, Everett Grimm, were shooting their BB guns in the woods nearby when they stumbled across two abandoned puppies huddled together under a pile of leaves. I saw them as they approached our house and went running to meet them. When I saw the pups, it was love at first sight. After asking Bob lots of questions about them, I asked the most important one.

"Do you think Mom and Dad will let us keep him?" I had already taken a liking to the tiny gray one with brown speckles on his nose. His hair was matted and dirty, but I ignored that as I cuddled the helpless, whimpering little creature in my arms.

"Mom might be okay with it, but Dad will probably say no. He doesn't want animals of any kind in the house."

"That's not fair," I whined. "Finders, keepers and besides, you can't take them back. They'll die."

Everett spoke up. "Let's give them names. That might make it harder for our parents to say no. I'm calling mine Little Duke."

That was a perfect name for the brown pup. He was the smaller and feistier of the two. He yipped and yapped constantly and never quit scratching. One of his ears looked like it had been chewed on and the other one stuck straight up.

"Let's call ours Prince," I announced. "That way they sound like they belong together." Bob agreed.

We assumed guardianship and now it remained for us to sell our mother on the idea of having a pet underfoot. If we could convince her, we knew our father would be hard-pressed to refuse. Everett took Little Duke home and we went looking for Mom. She was in the kitchen peeling potatoes for supper.

"Look at what we found," Bob said, as he held up the pup. "His name is Prince. Everett found one too. Is it okay if we keep him—please?" Mom put the peeler down, wiped her hands on her apron and took the pup. She gave one of those half-smiles and a sigh that told us she was on our side, but was quick to caution us.

"He certainly is cute, but don't get your hopes up. You know how your dad is about pets, but if he says yes, then it will be fine with me too."

It was typical of her to be so understanding. She went to the refrigerator for a bottle of milk and poured some into a bowl. "He looks like he could use a little nourishment," she said as she stroked his head.

We were excited to have Mom's approval, but convincing our father would be more difficult so we plotted a different approach—one that would stir his compassion instead of his logic. We decided to give Prince a makeover. We gave him a warm sudsy bath in a washtub in the basement, then we dried him and brushed him until his coat was sleek and shiny. For the finishing touch, we splashed some of Dad's Bay Rum After Shave on him to mask any doggie odor. Satisfied, we headed for the back-porch swing. With all of the pampering we had given him, Prince was content. He snuggled between us and fell asleep. At 5:30, Dad came home. We heard Mom talking with him for what seemed like forever. She was making a case for having a family pet and pointing out that we were old enough to accept the responsibility. Then the screen door swung open.

"I understand you want to keep your new friend," Dad said, looking a bit somber.

"Yes, Sir," we said in unison.

He leaned over to pet Prince. At that moment the pup opened his eyes, stretched and gave a big yawn. His timing was perfect. We figured Dad was weakening when he gave a hearty laugh at this stellar performance. He propped his hand under his chin to think about his answer and then gave us the one we wanted.

"I will agree, but only on several conditions. Having a pet requires a serious commitment. Are you willing to take full charge of him?"

Again we gave an eager, "Yes, Sir."

"Let's see if you can keep your word without causing any work for your mother or me. He will have to stay in the basement, so make sure you put a lot of newspapers down until he is housebroken. If he becomes a problem, you will have to find another home for him." Fair enough, we thought.

Bob and I were delirious. We were even happier when Everett returned to report that his parents had given him permission to keep Little Duke. Our world seemed perfect.

The days went by quickly. Instead of playing Monopoly or riding our bikes, we kept busy caring for the pups. Our parents were pleasantly surprised that we were being very responsible and keeping our promises. Little Duke and Prince scampered about in our backyards and got into plenty of mischief. They took a fancy to Mom's laundry basket, hiding under the sheets and towels as she took them off the clothesline. They also loved to chew on the spearmint leaves in her garden, much to her dismay. I especially enjoyed the messy pup kisses they nuzzled on my cheek when I fed them their treats. They had grown a little, but were still small, so we had to watch over them constantly. We stood a little taller with them being totally dependent on us. A new school year was around the corner and we were already dreading the thought of leaving them. And then the unthinkable happened.

Shortly after breakfast one morning, Everett pounded on our front door. I opened it to find him sobbing, holding Little Duke in his arms. The pup was limp.

"What happened?" I screamed. Bob and Mom came running when they heard me.

"I found him in the garden like this. I don't know how he got out. He's not breathing." Everett's eyes were pleading for help, but there was nothing anyone could do. Little Duke was dead. With as much calm as she could muster, Mom went into the kitchen and returned with a tea towel. She bent over the pup, gently wrapped him in it and handed him back to Everett.

"Let's take him to your place," she said, "I need to talk with your mother."

Our eyes were blinded with tears as we took the brief walk up the alley. Mrs. Grimm met us with a sympathetic smile and open arms. She led us into the kitchen, took Little Duke from her distraught son and carried the pup into the next room. When she came back, she did what moms are masterful at doing when aid and comfort are required. She reached for the cookie jar.

"Let's take a few minutes to eat these cookies and then we can decide what to do."

She poured a glass of milk for each of us. Both moms hovered about, taking time to give much-needed hugs. Our salty tears mingled with the sugary crunch of Mrs. Grimm's "mystery cookies." (We called them that because she was a frugal woman and would add whatever was in her cupboard to stretch the cookie dough). After we had our fill, Everett spoke up.

"I want to have a real funeral for Little Duke and I want everyone to do something special." And so, we were given assignments—the moms were included.

We prepared for the wake. First, we darkened the dining room by drawing the drapes. Then we lit candles and placed them on the sideboard, along with some dandelions I put in a Mason jar. Everett emptied a Nabisco Graham Cracker box, lined it with the tea towel my mother had donated and laid the pup inside. The glow of the candles flickered around his lifeless form. We succumbed to the solemnity of the moment with uncontrollable sobs.

Mrs. Grimm had the ministerial duties. She opened her Bible to the 23rd Psalm and began, "The Lord is my Shepherd, I shall not want." That was all she could do. Her voice faded and she did a lot of swallowing. She came down with some kind of an affliction that we later called "the shakes." She leaned over, clutched her stomach and put her hand to her mouth. Her shoulders heaved up and down, but she never made a sound. Just when it seemed she would start to recover, it would strike again. However, after a lot of starts and stops and to our relief, she finally got to the "Amen."

My mom was asked to do the eulogy. Considering how little she had to do with either Prince or Little Duke, she was at a loss for words, but she managed to get out, "He was a good dog." Suddenly, "the shakes" overtook her too.

Then it was my turn. With the bravado of a mezzo-soprano, I belted out my version of "The Old Rugged Cross." By this time, both moms were red in the face and reaching for the box of Kleenex. They were completely overcome with grief.

One at a time, we filed past the paper coffin to say our goodbyes. Everett placed a small Milk Bone at the tip of the pup's nose. Wherever Doggie Heaven was, he would arrive with his treat. Everett ceremoniously closed the lid and secured it with gobs of Scotch Tape. Then he tenderly picked up Little Duke and moved towards the back stairs that led down to the garden. Bob followed, holding a little wooden cross that he had hastily made with his wood burning set. I was next, rendering the second verse to the only hymn I knew. The procession made its way with Mrs. Grimm and Mom bringing up the rear. There was still no sound from either of them.

When we got to the garden, Everett placed the box in the hole he had dug under the grape arbor. He and Bob shoveled the dirt on top of it and marked the grave with the cross to commemorate Little Duke's final resting place.

"Ashes to ashes and dust to dust," Everett said, choking back tears. "And now a moment of silence."

We bowed our heads and then the three of us hummed "Taps." At the conclusion of the service, we returned to the kitchen and ate more mystery cookies to nurse our broken hearts, spinning tales of our adventures with the pups and wallowing in our grief.

A few days later, Prince found his way out of our house. We searched relentlessly for him, but he was never seen again. Our sorrow was multiplied. We consoled ourselves with the belief that some kind person would love him as much as we did and give him another happy home. Bob and Everett were brave. I wasn't. I cried for days, missing all the fun we had and the joy that the pups had given us.

Time hasn't diminished the clarity of that day. Everett stays in touch from his home in Coos Bay, Oregon and we still savor the memory of those sweet little puppies. To this day, every time I go back to Natrona Heights, I drive past the Grimms' home. They are gone, the grape arbor is gone. There is only the reminder of a childhood awakening that became a bridge to becoming an adult.

I cherish the grace and humor that our moms offered as they helped us step into a larger world. They let us experience change and the uncertainties of life, but not alone. Their tender love and nurturing have enabled me to raise my two sons, following the same path. I've had my own bouts of the shakes with some of their mishaps. I've learned too that hugs served with my mystery cookies have helped to soothe and calm them from things of which childhoods are made.

Even today, when those times come around that wound and sadden me, it is a comfort to reach back and remember that the ache in my heart now is the same as it was then.

Rest in peace, Little Duke.

Michael, the Prince

By jd young

I had been princess then started hearing each night
A Prince was soon arriving - all had better be right
The house to be cleaned, his room to be set
Clothing folded, nappies done – clean bassinette
When his majesty arrived we all breathed well
He was 9 months coming and we had lived through hell
The fuss, muss and bother that we prayed to survive
Was finally resolved when the Prince arrived
He was to be last, though docs had said that before
Thus he was dressed in the finest from the Robert Hall store
We 9 sat at the table, he seated on his throne
We gagged on peas & carrots while he munched on what he chose
He grew not so tall but his personality excelled
He determined his future before he could spell
Fame, fortune and wealth were his only aspiration
The Prince would excel regardless of the situation
He flourished despite odds the meek would not have survived
And seized upon all duties that would make him thrive
As a busboy he started but quickly advanced
Lead waiter, head concierge he left nothing to chance
Head of food and beverage and then sales as well
We stopped keeping track – us ne'r do wells
New cars, spacious homes and clothing he amassed
In ground pools, cheeky art and men to cut the grass
Hugo Boss and Armani forever drape his frame
Clois du Bois & Johnny Black are his stock & trade
He continues to climb the stairs of success
We love him yet admit some jealousy exists
We forgive him as always for we all know
He's paying for this party - and our rooms as well.

Modified Softball

By William R. Byrne

The play ball came streaking in towards home plate, fast and outside. It was a total sucker pitch, but I couldn't resist. I swung as hard and far as my eight-year-old arms could reach. Miraculously, the wooden bat made contact, a glancing blow off the bottom of the plastic sphere. The ball lurched upward, corkscrewing into the gap between second and third base.

Tommy Robinson tensed, hands raised in anticipation as he tracked the ball from beneath the visor of his Orioles cap. He underestimated the spin. His easy popfly was now a Mexican jumping bean, careening from hand to chest and then out of his clutches as it shot over his head, knocking his hat to the grass.

As Tommy juggled, I sprinted. I was across the Frisbee first base before he could scoop the ball off the lawn.

"SAFE!" I shouted, my lungs bursting with delight at having cheated the typically sure handed fielding of my neighborhood nemesis.

Tommy glared at me, his fierce blue eyes burning with contempt. "You'll never make it to second alive." His threat carried the kind of authority that two years in seniority and two inches in height conveyed among adolescent boys. He palmed the ball and slapped it menacingly against his free hand before flipping it back to my sister on the pitcher's mound.

The sixties were an era before working moms where June to August was an endless summer of hot, humid days whose monotony was only rarely interrupted by a week of family vacation or day camp. Once the novelty of school's joyful end had faded, all the kids of our neighborhood faced a common enemy - boredom. In our idyllic Baltimore suburban community of Fellowship Forest, the least common denominator solution to pass an afternoon was to choose up sides for nine innings of modified softball.

"Modified" softball was played according to traditional baseball rules, with one important exception. In our version of the national pastime, a plastic play ball, the kind sold out of big wire bins at the grocery store, was substituted for the baseball. This larger ball was the great equalizer, leveling the playing field across age groups. Its size made it easy for younger kids to hit and impossible for older ones to knock out of the park.

Keeping me company at first base for the opposition was Sally Hicks. In my young eyes, Sally was an exotic older woman, a thirteen year old blue-eyed brunette with cute, page boy bangs. My sister Anne was on the pitcher's mound. A new teenager herself, she was tall and slender, not quite a tomboy, but willing and able to challenge her male peers in sports. The previously introduced Tommy Robinson lurked at short stop. His buddy Larry Sturm guarded shallow center. Larry and Tommy were both ten years old; Tommy quick and lean, Larry hefty and strong. Pat Robinson, one of Tommy's four older brothers, manned the outfield with my older brother Connell.

Today's contest was being played on a Saturday afternoon in the Robinson's front yard. We rotated between this location, their backyard and our backyard to keep from beating the grass in the baselines to death.

As the youngest player in the game, I was thrilled to be included, much less on base. For as long as I could remember, I'd suffered through the humiliation of the "NC" or "No-Count" designation. "NC" is what the older kids whispered when the little kids came to bat. It was a spiteful accommodation of parental management's insistence that the big kids let the little ones join in their games. As a "No Count," you were allowed to hit and run the bases, but your outs and runs didn't matter. Today I was playing for real. I wanted to score!

Tommy's older sibling Michael, third from the top of the Robinson brothers, strutted to the plastic garbage can lid home plate. Michael was the stockiest of his family and he was not opposed to throwing his weight around when it suited him.

"I'm going to make you pay for that error, Tommy," Michael told his brother, pointing his bat Babe-Ruth like towards deep center.

Michael bounced Anne's first pitch foul into the driveway. Tommy watched her chase after the ball. He had the boyish family freckles of his brother Michael and the tough athleticism of his brother Pat. With four big brothers I suspect Tommy often got knocked around at home. I truly regretted that situation, as it left me, and sometimes my brother Connell, as the next step down in the neighborhood food chain. Tommy had a lot of adolescent angst, and my brother and I bore the brunt of it.

I tensed as my sister's next pitch sailed high and wide. Don Hicks, Sally's older brother, covered as catcher even though he was on our team. Don had dark hair like his sister, buzz cut short like all the Robinsons. He tossed the ball back to Anne.

"C'mon, get one over the plate. We're falling asleep back here," Don shouted.

I stayed close to first, watching Michael as he twirled the tip of the bat behind his head. My attention then moved to Tommy. Our eyes met. He sneered. I winced. He was thinking force out.

"Michael, bring me home!" I squeaked with as much testosterone as I could muster.

Michael swatted the next pitch sharply over Tommy's head into shallow left. I was off like the metal rabbit at the greyhound races the instant the ball hit the ground. Tommy ran back for the ball as I rounded second base. I could see him sweep it up, turn and take two great leaps towards me as I dove into third. My outstretched hand clutched the base at the same moment I felt the sting of the ball on the back of my exposed left calf.

60

Point of information – it was perfectly legal and encouraged to throw a base runner out in modified softball by drilling them with the ball.

"Out," Tommy yelled triumphantly.

"Safe," Michael rebutted from first base. A chorus of "Safe by a mile," and "Tie goes to the runner," echoed from my teammates behind home plate.

"I nailed him on the leg," Tommy insisted. He marched toward me, finger pointing accusatorily.

A red splotch confirmed visually what my tingling skin told me was a foregone conclusion. Yes, he most certainly had nailed me. But possession was nine-tenths of the law. With one foot rooted to the hallowed sanctuary of third base, I stood my ground.

"You were out," Tommy said. He drove the point home with a chest-deflating poke to my solar plexus.

"Leave him be," Michael yelled at his brother.

I leaned back, putting as much distance between myself and Tommy as I could while keeping one toe on the base. Playing in the big leagues, I thought to myself as I rubbed my chest, could really hurt.

Don tried to settle the issue by taking his place at the plate. "Batter up," he called, waving my sister to proceed with the game.

Anne looked at Tommy, then to Pat in the outfield.

"Oh forget it, Tommy," Pat said. Pat was not only faster than his brothers, he was also smarter. "I'm not standing here while you idiots argue. Play or I'm leaving."

"Bunch of cheaters," Tommy muttered. He bounced the ball at Anne and sulked back to his position. Anne turned to face the next batter.

Her first pitch came in low and short, rolling over home plate.

"Kick ball was yesterday, girlie." Don stepped forward and booted the ball back to my sister.

Her next pitch was higher, and not surprisingly, way inside. If you could throw a play ball fast enough to intentionally hurt a batter, Don Hicks would have been flat on his back.

Don ducked his head clear of my sister's bean ball. Donna Morlock, another of my sister's neighborhood friends, awkwardly tossed the ball back to my sister. Donna hated sports and threw like a girl, but she was in love with Don Hicks.

Anne's next pitch was in the sweet spot but Don swung too early. He lined it to the foul side of first base where it lodged ominously in the bushes at the corner of the Robinson's driveway and the street.

A communal groan rose from fielders and batter alike. Not the bushes!

When a baseball hits a neighbor's window, the window comes out on the short end. Not so with a play ball and a sticker bush.

"Great shot, Don," Michael said, walking to the bushes from first base. He eased the ball from its nest among the spine covered branches and raised it to one ear to listen for the telltale hiss of escaping air.

"Will the patient live, Doctor?" Don asked.

"I give him a minute, maybe two," Michael answered. "Barely enough time," he paused, "for revenge against its *murderer*," he accused, throwing the ball wildly at his team mate.

Don's arms sprung up to deflect Michael's strike, bouncing the ball across the yard.

"Keep away!" Michael shouted as he chased down the ball. He grabbed it and tossed it back to Don. Pat charged in from the outfield, tackling Michael to the ground after he released the ball.

My sister locked both her hands on Don's throwing arm before he had the chance to find an open receiver. Michael and Pat rolled around on the grass in a tumble of arms and legs. Donna came to Don's aid, tickling Anne at the waist in an effort to win his freedom.

One-handing the rapidly shrinking ball with his free left hand, Don flipped it towards me. I caught in on the fly, tucking it into my breadbox.

Concentrating on the ball, I'd lost track of my coverage. Tommy came out of nowhere, hitting me high and hard. Wrapping his arms around my chest, he energetically body slammed me into the turf. I hit shoulder first, the pain of the contact quickly diverted by the oppressive weight of my attacker steadily squeezing the air out of my lungs.

"Give it up," Tommy said, his stronger arms reaching round my collapsed form to pry the ball free. He then twisted around, the two of us back to back on the lawn, me on the bottom eating grass while he boastfully waved his prize.

"Our ball now," Tommy said, leaning harder into my back as I gasped for breath.

Michael and Pat were still entangled but now mobile, lurching steadily towards us on their knees. Michael was fixed mongoose-like to Pat's back, immobilizing his brother's arms in a full nelson. Pat slithered forward, struggling to break free. Don too was rushing to join the melee, escaping my sister's clutches just as Michael and Pat came crashing into the pile.

The next few minutes were a wild free-for-all, the five of us wrestling and jabbing for domination. Well, it was for four of us anyway. I was simply trying to stay alive beneath the mayhem transpiring above me.

Don escaped first, leaving the Three Stooges to duke it out until we ran out of gas.

Michael was by now sitting on Pat, who was sitting on Tommy who was sitting on me. Eventually, they dragged themselves away to lick their wounds and began to discuss the next stage of the afternoon's entertainment.

"Anybody else have a ball?" Michael asked as he examined the deflated remains of the sticker bushes' latest victim.

"Wiffle ball?" Connell asked. "I know we have one of those."

"Or spud," Donna added.

The conversations quickly diverged along traditional lines and cliques. Without the unifying focus of our game, we dispersed into our own backyard Tower of Babel, Donna, Sally and Anne clumping off on their own while the boys divided up between younger and older.

Everyone that is, except for me. I lay motionless, arms and legs spread eagle on the lawn as I stared silently skyward.

"Bill, are you okay?" My sister asked. She walked over for a closer look. Soon the others followed until the whole gang circled me with the anxious looks of a bunch of cowboys standing over a downed calf.

Anne knelt beside me. "What's wrong?"

"I'm not sure," I said. "It really hurts when I move."

"C'mon let's help him up," Michael volunteered. He and my sister slipped their arms under my shoulders from opposite sides and gently lifted.

"Ohhhhh, stop."

They froze, held me for a moment longer; then eased me back to the ground.

"God, you're such a little faker," Tommy announced, rolling his eyes and stepping away before collapsing to the ground. "Help me, help me, I have a broken neck."

"Give it a rest, Tommy," Michael said. As the oldest present, Michael knew he'd be in the hot seat if I were seriously injured. As the biggest, he further knew that he stood a better than average chance of being tagged with the blame for having sat on top of the pile.

"Let's try again," he suggested.

This time he and Anne took it slower, but every inch electrified my upper back and left shoulder with dizzying pain. "No, no, stop," I cried, urging them to reverse direction. They slowly lowered me back onto the soothing green carpet of the lawn.

"Is he paralyzed?" Donna asked.

"Brain dead maybe," Anne teased, feeling the weak grasp of my hand in hers, "but probably not paralyzed."

"Can you try one more time?" my sister encouraged.

I raised one knee, then straightened the leg, then did the same to the other, confirming if only for myself that there was hope that I would one day walk again. Encouraged by this success, I tried to lift my upper body on my own, managing to tip my good right shoulder several inches before hitting a wall of pain for the third time.

"I can't do it. It hurts too much."

I smiled wanly. As long as I wasn't moving, I felt fine.

"Connell, go get Dad," Anne said.

Connell trotted off across the Robinson's driveway toward our house next door.

"What happened?" Anne asked.

"I don't know. Tommy crashed into me and then we were all wrestling."

"It's not my fault," Tommy said..

"Calm down. No one is blaming you." Michael told his brother. "Not yet, anyway," he let slip under his breath.

"Did you pull a muscle?" My sister asked, reaching around to gently massage my neck. I tensed when her fingers worked their way across the top of my tender shoulder.

"Right around there, that's where it hurts."

"Hmmm, maybe he broke his shoulder," Donna suggested.

"Damn," Michael grumbled. "My Mom's gonna be pissed."

"Heartwarming as your concern may be," Anne said, "let's see what my Dad has to say first."

The initial curiosity over my injury not having been satisfied with massive blood loss or exposed bone, the rest of the gawkers had by now dispersed. Michael too soon wandered off, leaving only my sister at my side. I overheard Tommy talking about tether ball. The girls headed to Sally's house.

"What's taking Dad so long!" Anne asked, looking towards our house. She wanted to dart off with her friends, but for the moment, sisterly concern kept her at my side.

I too was wondering about the delay. It had been ten, maybe fifteen minutes since Connell left. It didn't hurt if I kept still, but I was getting bored. And a little itchy.

Finally, Anne spotted our brother working his way down the hill to us. When he arrived, she asked about Dad.

"Did you tell him?"

"Yes, I told him." Connell said. "I told him Bill was hurt."

"Well," Anne said, standing up. "What did he say?" She looked at Connell and then back up to the house, "Is Dad coming?"

""I don't know, I mean, I'm not sure," he explained, "He was taking a nap on the couch. It was kind of hard to understand him. I think he wants Bill to come up to the house."

"Come up to the house? How? On a stretcher!?" Anne fumed.

She stood for a moment, fists clenched at the sides of her cutoff jean shorts.

"You two," she said, pointing to my brother and me, "stay here. I'll wake him up!" With that, she marched off to the house.

Connell dropped to the ground, sitting Indian style next to me. "Feeling better?" He asked.

"Sure," I said. "Go get Tommy. Maybe he wants to break my other shoulder."

"Wow, you really think you broke your shoulder?" His imagination was racing. "I'll draw something really cool on your cast," he offered. "What do you want, a Tyrannosaurus Rex? A spaceship?"

The minutes dragged on and still no sign of Dad or Anne. Surprisingly, some relief did emerge from the Robinson's porch in the form of Pat bearing a paper cup of lemonade.

"Here, have some of this," Pat offered. I turned my head sideways to half sip, half dribble the cool, sweet refreshment.

"Mrs. Forney wants to know if you are okay."

I glanced up towards their screened in front porch, vaguely discerning the slight frame of the Robinson's elderly babysitter through the window. She waved. I raised my good hand in a signal back.

Mrs. Forney was Mrs. Robinson's General Patton in the daily battle to maintain order in a household where she was outnumbered seven to one. In a cruel twist of gender determination probability, all of Mrs. Robinson's six offspring were boys. On this particular Saturday morning Mrs. Forney was holding the fort alone, neither of the Robinson parents was home. In keeping with Mrs. Forney's law of the land, the boys were not allowed to have friends in the house. In fact, the Robinson boys in general were not welcome in the house on a fine day such as this. Apparently this rule had an unexplained corollary that she never left the house, as she did not venture forth first hand to learn why one of the neighborhood children had been laid out on her lawn for the last hour. She'd dispatched Pat to do the reconnaissance.

"So, is anyone coming to help," Pat asked.

"Anne went to get Dad," Connell said.

Pat tipped me another sip of lemonade then handed the cup to Connell. "I'll tell Mrs. Forney," he said, and was gone.

The porch door opened, held by a steely, age-spotted arm. Connell and I watched Mrs. Forney debrief her scout; then they both disappeared into the house.

"Well, at least we won't die of thirst," Connell said, drinking the remainder of my lemonade. "Oooops," he smiled. "Did you want some more?"

I extended my right fist in a weak punch to his thigh. A single jolt of agony rippled outward from the base of my neck down the entire side of my upper body.

"Uhhggg," I groaned. "No more moving for me."

A few quiet minutes passed before Connell spotted the rescue party. "Look, here they come," he said, pointing towards our back yard.

A minute later, my father was standing over me with a look of concern. At six feet, Dad always towered over us, but from flat on my back on the ground, he seemed taller than ever. He wore a dark blue Banlon shirt, pressed tan dress pants and brown loafers. His utilitarian flat top crew cut was barber shop fresh. Black, horned-rim glasses were folded into the pocket of his shirt.

He knelt down, gently running his fingers through the hair on my forehead. "Your sister thinks you broke your shoulder," Dad said. "Does it hurt?"

"Only if I try to sit up," I said.

"He got crunched at the bottom of a pile-on," Connell added.

My father looked around. "A pile-on?"

"A game of keep away," Anne explained. "Everyone has fled the scene of the crime."

"Sorry for the delay," Dad said.

"He'd still be on the couch if Mrs. Forney hadn't called on the phone," Anne blurted out.

Dad silenced her with a raised eyebrow. "Let's say she shared her concern with me directly and leave it at that," Dad said. "The question now is; what to do about you, young man. We can't have you lazing around out here until your mother comes home."

Obviously, Mom was not home. She'd have been at my side instantly if she'd been within a mile's radius. Emergency medical care was her department. Dad was clearly out of his element here, and all of us knew it.

"Do you think you can make it home if we help?"

"It really hurts when I sit up," I insisted. "But I'll try again."

One strong arm slipped around my back from my good right side. It hurt every bit as much as before, if not more, when he lifted for the first few inches. But then the pain eased, and once I made it fully sitting upright on the lawn, I felt no discomfort whatsoever.

"It hurt for a minute, but now its better," I said with great relief.

"That's a good start. Well done," Dad said. "Take a minute to relax and then we can try to get you on your feet."

I took a few deep breaths; then nodded my head. "I'm ready to try."

My father stood behind me, bracing each of my sides with his hands. I leaned forward as he lifted, careful to keep the pressure at my waist. A moment later, I was standing, finally freed from my grassy prison.

"There you go," Dad said. "Good as new."

I did feel good for a few seconds. Then the bottom fell out. I went dizzy and slumped back against him, the pressure of his chest against my injured shoulder once again lighting up my nervous system with agonizing flashes of pain.

"Ohhhhhhh," I moaned.

"I've gotcha," Dad said, bracing me against himself as one arm slipped down behind my knees. With his other arm firmly around my back, he lifted me as he stood. "Maybe a ride home would be a better idea."

My father was more lean than muscular, but he bore my weight effortlessly. Still, with each step across the Robinson's driveway and up the hill through our back yard, hot streaks cut through my left shoulder.

"Not much farther," he encouraged as we reached our driveway. I buried my head in his neck to hide from the pain, the scent of his Old Spice aftershave flooding my senses.

"Anne," he said, "open the car door."

My father eased me into the passenger side of his car. The landing was rough, but once settled into an upright sitting position and no longer moving I regained some level of comfort.

"You did fine," Dad told me.

"Anne, help him with the seatbelt, will you?" He instructed. "I need to grab my wallet and leave a note for Mom."

Dad went off to the house while my sister reached gingerly around and behind, feeling for the bulky metal seatbelt clasps of the ancient Chevy. "I'm surprised they even had seatbelts when they built this thing," she said.

Anne and Connell tried to amuse me with tales of their personal experiences with hospitals. Connell was the expert here, a veteran of open-heart surgery when he was only five years old.

"Hopefully, they won't cut you up like this," he boasted, raising his t-shirt to expose the fat, purple earthworm of a scar that stretched horizontally across the length of his chest. "Fifty stitches! Top that!"

"You are so gross," Anne said. "He is going in for a broken shoulder, not a heart transplant, Dr. Frankenstein!"

Mercifully, Dad soon returned to save me from this cheery repartee.

"I called Mrs. Forney and filled her in," he told Anne. If you and Connell need anything before Mom gets home, go over to the Robinsons. I left your Mother a note on the kitchen table. Tell her I will try to call in an hour. That would be," he said, looking at his watch, "around three o'clock. She and your sister should be back from shopping by then. I'm taking your brother to the emergency room at St. Joe's. Tell her to wait till I call so we can decide how best to meet up."

Once he was settled in and ready to begin the ride to the hospital, my dad paused and looked across the bench seat to me.

"Feeling better? Up for a little drive?"

"It doesn't hurt much while I am sitting here," I said.

"Sure you are up for the ride to the hospital?"

I had no idea where he was heading with this. If I said no, was he going to call an ambulance?

"I'm sure Dad," I said. "As long as I don't have to use my left arm to hitchhike, I think I'll make it."

He smiled and nodded. "Good to hear. One last thing before we leave," he said.

My father leaned forward, pulling his thick black wallet out of the back pocket of his slacks. He fished around inside, then pulled out a ten-dollar bill.

My eyes widened. Ten dollars was more money than the average eight year old could imagine in 1968. I think we

70

were getting about a quarter a week for our allowance back then, so ten dollars was three years' worth of taking out the trash and cleaning bathrooms!

Why was he showing me a ten dollar bill?

"What if I was to say to you;" my father asked, "that you could keep this ten dollar bill if you could pick it up off the dashboard." He set the bill down.

I stared longingly at the proffered reward, then uncertainly at the appendage hanging lifelessly from my left shoulder. It had been ten minutes since I'd settled into the car and it really hadn't hurt much at all since then. Maybe, just maybe, it was only bruised. A bruise can't hurt forever, I hoped.

But first, I had another thought.

I stared my Dad straight in the eye, scrunched up my face in a contortion of determination, and slowly but surely began to raise my right hand. Veins popping from my neck in superhuman concentration, it climbed slowly higher toward the glove box.

"Not that hand," my father whispered with a wink. "The hurt one, if you can."

Busted!

I smiled sheepishly; then gently stretched my neck slowly from side to side. Not quite so far to the left, because it still really hurt. Not an encouraging sign.

Bracing myself for the jarring snap of a giant mouse trap springing closed on my upper arm and shoulder, I tentatively raised my left hand. Sure enough, an inch or two out of my lap was all I could muster before blaring sirens of pain began ringing through my head. I wavered, reaching over with my right hand to steady my left before my father threw in the towel.

"Okay, no higher, Bill."

He wrapped my left hand in his own; then slowly lowered it to my lap. "Son, I think that we need to have a doctor check out that shoulder."

I shrugged. Even that hurt. "Yeah, I guess you're right."

"Here," he said, folding up the ten dollar bill and stuffing it in my shirt pocket. "That's for trying."

After several tedious hours in the waiting room, a few pokes from the doctor, and a trip to the X-Ray lab, the verdict was in. Dad and I returned home around dinnertime not with an awe inspiring cast, but an awkward wrap-around sling. I'd broken my collarbone. This was a great disappointment. The broken collarbone is the booby prize of broken bones. Not quite as lame as a broken toe, but nowhere near the status symbol of a broken arm. You can't tap annoyingly on the kitchen table waiting for dinner with a sling, much less smash a Lego city in Godzilla-like rage. The injury kept me on the modified softball disabled list for six weeks.

That summer passed, then the fall, then the winter and then many more seasons and years. I often wonder what my father's recollection of that afternoon might have been had we had the opportunity to reminisce about it over a beer or two as we watched my children play on a lazy summer afternoon. If fate had been more generous with our time together, perhaps this memory might have faded among the many new weekend adventures with Grandpa that my son, daughter and I might have shared together.

My Wonderful World

By Mary Ellen Gavin

Childhood memories for me go back to my high chair days and looking out at all the people bustling around our kitchen. Being the youngest of five, lots of folks populated our home along with visitors from early morning till way after midnight. These happy faces chatted, laughed and sang. Who needed television when I had this cast of characters to entertain me?

My maternal country relatives from the South visited early in the day to reminisce over dark coffee and my mother's famous date nut bread. They mused about living "down south" vs. "the big city." There was one aunt who, when it was time to leave, had a habit of standing up and reciting, "And the South shall rise again."

My paternal Chicago relatives still held to their European, mainly British, traditions and came for afternoon tea and family gossip. I can still see the white cardboard boxes of German, Italian or French pastries coming in the door from the fine bakeries so prevalent back then. The more grease spots, the more sweet rolls inside.

While preparing for supper, Big Band tunes played from the living room's Victrola. My teenage sisters jitterbugged around the kitchen as they set down dishes and silverware. My brother, and always a pal or two, ran around trying to snitch food. Gathering around the table could go casual with lots of joking, or extremely formal if my father was present. After the table was cleared, my sisters sang harmony 'alla' the Andrew Sisters while washing dishes over the porcelain sink with a checkered skirt.

With so much fun going on around me, I couldn't wait to get out of the high chair.

By the time I was five, my life centered on playing outdoors with the pack of kids who lived in our mammoth apartment building that we considered our castle. Starting early, first one up and out began calling for the others. No, we were not allowed to ring bells or knock on doors. Those intrusions were considered impolite and might disturb parents, or worse grandparents. Instead, we cupped our hands and called out, "Yo Oh, Patsy!" Or, "Yo, Oh, Sylvia!" The Albert sisters lived above me and I loved them both.

By the time we rounded up our gang, some already had ideas about what we would do that day. Playing baseball in the empty lot behind our building was always a priority. Although the lot belonged to our building, it was not maintained. Broken glass and dog dirt had to be cleared before we could start sliding into our wooden crate bases.

Mr. Green was our nemesis. He was a cranky old man who owned a nasty old dog and they both lived in the house next to the empty lot. Say goodbye to any ball sailing into his yard because that mad mutt, Whitey, patrolled his fence line like a Nazi. A few of the kids were already wearing bite scars on their calves from trying to retrieve their ball while bragging that Whitey was too slow to catch them.

We long suspected that Mr. Green allowed Whitey to do his business in the lot and I must confess that a few of us might have thrown what we found on the ground right back over the fence. Whitey, a bull or pug, liked to bite and only obeyed Mr. Green. Patsy warned us that Whitey had changed his tactics. When an errant ball flew across, he acted aloof, but we were not fooled.

One hot afternoon, the ball that belonged to our best player, Patrick Woods, went flying into "Green Land." Tall and thin, Patrick was a cocky kid. He eyed Whitey languishing at the far end of the yard and smiled. "I'm going over. Whitey's fat and old. I can outrun him."

We gathered around our pal, reminding him of prior run-ins with Whitey where kids came out bleeding. Patsy, our most respected member, stepped forward and said, "I was holding this for a surprise, but my mother is willing to take us girls to Riverview Park tomorrow. And Patrick, if you get your ball back, I'll ask if you can come too."

Patrick licked his lips as he began scaling the fence in his high-top black canvas shoes. Standing on the top of the wooden fence, he covered his eyes from the sun Indian Style and studied the snoozing dog. Turning back to us, Patrick put his finger to his lips, motioning for us to stay quiet. We nodded and shook our fists in the air, signaling solidarity.

Patrick jumped down on Mr. Green's thick green grass and froze. Whitey didn't move. Nobody moved. Eyes now on his ball waiting across the yard, Patrick took off. Dashing over rocks and through flowerbeds, he did not see that cagey canine's eyes pop open. We did, and someone near me whistled, "Patrick's a GONER!"

Whitey jumped up and let out one ferocious bark and the second floor window sprang open. The old geezer's head poked out, already cussing and swearing. "What the hell's going on out there?" He spotted us huddling in the empty lot and his face turned beet red. "You kids teasing Whitey again?"

Patsy spoke up, "Just looking at your pretty flowers."

Mr. Green turned his head away from Patrick to look at Patsy. "Don't ya be lookin' at my flowers."

Patrick was bent over his ball, frozen now in a silent standoff with Whitey, while Patsy continued to smooth talk Old Man Green. "My mother says you have the prettiest flowers on the block."

"What would YOUR MOTHER know about flowers?"

"She likes the deep pastel colors in your garden."

Mr. Green grunted in disgust, pulled his head in still mumbling about his flowers and slammed the window.

Patrick took off running with Whitey hot on his tail, snapping at the bottom of his blue jeans. Throwing his ball for Patsy to catch, he quickly scaled the fence. Instead of jumping down, he turned around to smile down at the barking dog and beat his chest like King Kong.

We cheered! Patrick jumped to our turf as Mr. Green yelled out the window again, "Why is Whitey BARKING?"

Patsy gave him another sweet smile, "Whitey wants to play with us, Mr. Green."

"No, he doesn't. Whitey HATES you kids. He'd like me to serve you up for his supper!" The window slammed back down again and we all stood there feeling the same horror.

The following morning all five of us: Patsy and Sylvia Albert along with Patrick Woods and his kid sister Maureen assembled on the front sidewalk to accompany Mrs. Albert to eight-o'clock Mass. Holding hands and trailing behind, we made the trek to St. Alphonsus church, whispering and giggling all the way.

After the long Latin Mass, we skipped a block ahead of Mrs. Albert to get home, eat and change into play clothes. The plan was to be at the corner to catch the Belmont Avenue Streetcar in a half hour and ride it up to Western Avenue where Riverview Park waited for all kids.

Right on time, we all climbed aboard the red and gold streetcar with breakfast in our tummies and fresh-scrubbed smiles. The conductor pulled the hanging wooden handle. Clang! Clang! The screeching sound of metal wheels along the embedded track signaled we were off. We made our way to the golden metal benches where we bunched together letting Mrs. Albert sit alone for the short ride.

Moving away from Lake Michigan's shore to the edge of the Chicago River changed the smell of the air. I was reminded of a dreaded water ride I had heard about and quickly asked, "Tell me we are not going on the Tunnel of Love?"

Patrick was quick to say, "Only me with all you girls. Heck, NO!"

Patsy could always calm him down, "C'mon, it's a fun boat ride."

Sylvia and Maureen shouted, "Kissing!"

Patsy looked out the window. "Next stop is us."

The conductor hollered out, "Western Avenue. River-view Park!"

We jumped down in the middle of the street and ran to the sidewalk eager to get to the entrance. Holding hands, we followed Mrs. Albert into the park. Eyes wide, we stopped to look down the midway at the spectacle of fun awaiting us.

Tilt-A-Twirl was the first ride and there was no line. We ran up as the attendant unlocked the chain. The bottoms of our shoes slid on the greasy tracks as we ran to an empty car. One of the older kids grabbed my hand and all five of us piled in together.

"Sit in the center so you don't get thrown out!" Sylvia yelled to me as we felt the slow pull of the machinery starting to accelerate. Scooting close, we grabbed the metal bar and held on tight.

The screaming began even before the bumpy ups-and-downs pulled our car into circles. Surprisingly, I was one of the loudest to yell. What fun! Our car spun around the giant metal bolt as we rode the waves of motion. When the black leather top of each car lifted to cover our heads and shut out the light, SILENCE!

Speeding up, we were lucky to hold on as we fought off our fears of any creepy things crawling on us in the dark. Bugs, snakes and river rats were all rumored to hide on the rides, at least that was what I heard when we shared scary stories. Now we were flying around in total darkness with only slits of light sliding across the floor. My cornflakes wanted to climb up my throat. I prayed not to get sick.

Around and around we tilted and twirled until the big engine hissed, signaling it was no longer generating speed. Now, we were free flying, powered only by centrifugal force, and it felt heavenly. We leaned our bodies into each spin to keep our car moving as the ride slowed down. The tops opened and folded back. We all took a deep breath of fresh air as the ride slowed, feeling excited to have made it to the end, ALIVE!

Everyone clapped as was customary back then to show appreciation for a good ride, a good movie or a good parade passing by.

Patrick was the first to jump out and yell, "I love this place!"

Patsy gathered the kids together and led us to where Mrs. Albert stood waiting.

Maureen shouted, "Two more low rides and we're ready for our first coaster."

We rode the Caterpillar, another ride that flew around in a circle, and the Electric Cars where we bumped into each other. The five of us, Patrick the biggest and me the smallest, walked the midway acting goofy. We passed the Beer Garden and the Hawkers shouting, "Try your luck!" The only game we agreed to play was Skee Ball. Bowling small wooden balls into lopsided holes was harder than it looked.

Up ahead was the Silver Streak, our first high ride. The line was long, but no one pushed or shoved. We moved slowly and quietly saying our last prayers as we listened to the wooden coasters pounding down the rails around us. As each one flew by, we saw the riders holding their breath and keeping their eyes shut. When it became our turn to get in and pull the bar back, no one said a word.

We buzzed out of the station and started up the first and worst rise. There was no turning back. Our ascent, looking up from a ninety-degree angle, took us straight to the clouds. My hands perspired as I tried to contemplate how the sky was able to change colors.

"Open your eyes and look at the view!" Patsy screamed. I obeyed to be amazed at the dizzying sight of the park and surrounding rooftops. "Hold on. Here we go!"

My backside suddenly lifted and then hovered above the seat. Still hanging at the top, I could see that the front of the coaster was beginning to plummet. Pulled into the fast descent allowed gravity to push me back into the seat. My body bumped like a bag of bones until we hit bottom.

"Take a deep breath. We're going up again." Patsy patted my head.

Eyes closed, I panted like a dog and held on while the ride flew up and down through the curves and tunnels. Finally the brakes kicked in and we slowly pulled back to the platform. My legs felt like rubber when I tried to stand and I could hardly move them to exit the car.

Mrs. Albert waited with small cups of pop. "You kids must be thirsty."

Patsy warned, "Only sips, we don't want to throw up!"

The soda tasted cool and sweet under the sun now burning down on us. I pulled up the bottom of my revered Cubs tee and wiped off the salty sweat sticking to my face.

Patsy smiled at her little cluster of friends, "Who's ready for The Chutes?" Being well trained by the nuns, our arms shot up in unison. "Good, cause it's next."

We walked past the Shooting Galleries and more Carnival Games until we saw the Chute-The-Chutes. Big boats full of laughing riders were being raised on huge elevators at the back of the gigantic water slide.

One boat was mounting the top and we stopped to watch the rushing water slowly pull it forward off the elevator. All the happy faces suddenly stopped smiling. They looked around, questioning how high they were above the park. They looked down, questioning how far they had to slide down the chute in order to hit the water below.

Looking frightened now, they quickly grabbed the "chicken" bar and anxiously waited.

The boat slowly tipped forward, held in the air for a second before it rocked back unsteadily. Finally, it pitched forward again and began to plunge into a free fall. Silent screams could be seen all the way down. The boat hit the water, bounced up into the air and back down again into a big splash. Everyone got wet.

"I'm not going on that ride," I said. No one argued with me as we walked past the Chutes and felt the water spray come at us from other boats slamming down the chute.

Patsy picked up our pace and groaned, "No Chutes! And I guess the Bobs and the Parachute Drop are out too?" Her eyes did not look at me, as I was too little to go with her. "C'mon, I need to go on ONE high ride today!" She made the impassioned face of a Madonna and stared at her mother, but Mrs. Albert was already shaking her head. Patsy turned to our brave Patrick, "What about you?"

He must have realized now why he was invited to come along and stepped up to perform his duty. "I'll go on the Bobs with you, but no thanks on the Parachute ride."

They ran ahead to get into the long line. The three of us could only stare at the eleven-car coaster reported to drop eighty-five feet off the first rise and rumored to take off your head on the first hairpin curve if you did not crouch low.

Mrs. Albert found a bench where Sylvia, Maureen and I sat with her to await the return of Patsy and Patrick. It was not long before Sylvia stood up and pointed to the rising coaster. We all ran to the metal fence and waved, but no one waved back. Stricken faces, including our two friends, looked sad as the ride slowed atop the first hill.

Maureen spoke up. "Supposed to be a five second delay up there." There was no time to start counting because the rails began to rumble. The coaster was speeding down the tracks, coming straight at us. As soon as it hit bottom, everyone inside slouched down and ducked their heads preparing for the curve. Flying past us without a sound, they disappeared into the tunnel under the wooden maze and we never saw their coaster again.

It took Mrs. Albert to convince me that the coaster had not disappeared, taking with it our two friends. Good to her promise, she pointed to Patrick and Patsy stumbling out of the Bob's exit and looking very pale. Neither could talk as they gasped for air and wiped off their sweat.

We let them calm down, before we continued to walk along the midway. Patsy and Patrick walked together now as if they shared a common bond. For some reason, I envied their new closeness.

The Parachutes loomed in front of us. It was so spectacular that none of us could look away. We stopped to watch two riders sitting on a small board being pulled up wires. When they hit the top and began their descent, the parachute caught a gust of air, opened and slowed the freefall. Some parachutes never opened and those riders slid down the wires like greased lightning.

I wondered how anyone could be brave enough to go up on this ride. Still, I didn't want the day to end and asked, "Are there any more rides for kids?"

Sylvia spoke up, "Aladdin's Castle is right around the corner." We ran and found the giant man's devilish face plastered across the front of the gigantic castle. The mysterious entrance was hidden inside his curly mustache.

Lining up, we stayed together going through the rooms. First, were our crazy reflections from the distortion mirrors. Next, were the rooms with twirling wooden floor tiles and stairs that moved every which way.

I grabbed Patrick's hand and we ran quickly up to the next level where we found rooms with sliding floors, slanted at odd angles. Gravity forced us to hold the handrails and take baby steps. It was not easy to make our way to the next room where another off-kilter floor had to be navigated. Crossing the last slanted room, I heard a loud motor. "What's that?"

Patrick smiled, "It's the Barrel Ride."

"I don't like the sound of it."

He bent down. "It's okay. We'll get through it."

"No, I want to go back."

"We can't go back." He turned and I saw all the kids piling up behind us, waiting for us to get going.

We followed the ominous drum roll sound to the next room where a giant wooden barrel was spinning. The kids ahead of us tried to run through it. Some made it, while others only fell down.

When it became our turn, Patrick grabbed my hands, lifted me off the floor and I tiptoed in front of him.

Following the crowd, we stepped into a dark and narrow corridor that forced us to walk single space. Patrick stayed behind me and I kept bumping into the back of a teenage girl in front. "Sorry, there's no light in here."

It got even darker, making us use our hands to follow the walls. The group in front sped up and the group behind Patrick fell behind because we were now alone dealing with strange noises and bursts of air as we traversed even higher into the castle. Twists and turns and eerie far off voices were frightening.

"It's okay, just keep moving." Patrick kept saying.

Ahead of us now were new ominous sounds. BOOM, SWISH, BOOM! They kept repeating and getting louder. Finally, we stepped out of the tunnel and into the top of the building several stories high. People were already looking out of cracks in the wall to see the miniaturized world below. Patrick ran up to one and loved what he saw, but I refused.

"Patrick, what is that noise?"

Another kid heard my question and looked at me as if I just landed on the planet. "It's Aladdin's Magic Carpet!"

Patsy, Sylvia and Maureen must have been far behind us and never caught up as we waited two-by-two in line.

Moving closer, we heard the BOOM, SWISH, BOOM get even louder until we got to see people step inside the little room and disappear behind the magic door.

The attendant, dressed like one of Ali Baba's Thieves, opened the door and the inside was empty except for a leather bench attached to the wall. The two kids ahead of us could not wait to get inside and sit on the bench. Again the attendant closed the door, BOOM, and pulled the big lever, SWISH, and opened the door again, BOOM.

It was our turn to go inside. Patrick held me by the hand and practically pulled me inside. We sat on the bench and I saw the long carpet spinning on rollers below our feet. Like an abyss, it waited to swallow us up.

Before I could panic, the door slammed and the seat collapsed. We spilled onto the rolling carpet and were pulled into the darkness.

Patrick whispered, "Don't worry, it's going to be fun." And he began to sing, "WHEE!" Our bottoms glided over the roller humps moving us along, and my body fell into the rhythm of the flowing carpet. I too sang out with joy.

Far below a spec of light appeared. "What is that?"

"The end of the ride. Don't worry. More Thieves down there will grab our hands so we don't fall getting off."

I enjoyed the remainder of Aladdin's ride and soon we could see two attendants looking up at us. One of them yelled, "Get ready!" We held out our hands and jumped off.

Patrick pulled me through the metal turnstile and we watched until we saw our friends exit looking happy. Sylvia was excited, "Did you like this ride?"

"It's the best. Guess that's why it's the last," Patrick answered.

Hot dogs and ice cream stands waited at the front gate for the last of our money. I can still picture the five of us racing to see who could get there first.

Riverview Park closed in 1967, and now a tech school, police station and shopping center occupy its seventy-four acres.

Paradise Lost

By Melanie Florence

I was a scrawny, withdrawn ten-year-old when we moved into a bigger house in a different neighborhood. My mother was either pregnant with my fourth brother or just had him. It did not make much difference; the chaos at home seemed about the same with or without him. So I played outside after school to escape. That is how I came to know Mrs. Schneider.

I first met her two daughters, Mary and Deidre, when I was walking to school and they came out from the L-shaped house across the street. Walking to school together led to playing together. Then they invited me to go to their church.

At that time, my family did not go to church. It was probably too much to try to keep six young children quiet, but my mother scoffed at the Christian religion, anyway. She called it anti-female and a pacifier for the masses. However, I longed for the guidance and ritual church provided and going to the First Lutheran Church with the Schneider family satisfied that need.

Sunday morning began early. I needed time to braid my long, straight hair, buff my black patent leather shoes with petroleum jelly to make them shine, and select my cleanest, least-wrinkled dress. Therefore, I was often the first one downstairs. As I scrounged around for something to eat, I checked the cereal boxes first. If ants had invaded them, I went to Plan B. Dragging a chair to the refrigerator, I explored its top, hoping to find a chance donut that had fallen out of the box during my siblings' relentless rummaging. If my search turned out to be fruitless, I resorted to toast. Toast was my last choice because grubby hands trying to get past the crusts mangled the loaf, not to mention that grungy bread made toast unappetizing and the bent-up pieces got stuck in the toaster.

After my bite to eat, I made sure all buttons were buttoned and zippers were zipped before heading across the street to the Pine sol-and-lemon-furniture-polish smell of the Schneider house.

At church, I frequently ended up sitting next to Mrs. Schneider in the pew. During the sermon, she would put her arm around my waist, pressing me against her large-framed and muscular but yielding body. I snuggled close, relishing the attention and contact. After the service, they invited me to come home with them and share their big family meal.

I often stayed for the rest of the afternoon and sometimes also for supper. Afterwards, we watched Walt Disney and Bonanza. Mr. and Mrs. Schneider sat on the couch with little Willie between them while Mary, Deidre and I sat Indian style or knock-kneed on the carpet in front of them.

On snowy or rainy days, Mary, Deidre and I sat on the spotless living room carpet and built troll dollhouses and furniture out of cardboard boxes, bits of wood, cloth, and wallpaper scraps. We made a swimming pool from a kidney-shaped hospital tray that Mrs. Schneider brought home from her job as a nurse. When we finished for the day, we picked up our houses and put them on the credenza, knowing they would remain untouched until the next time we used them. I could never do that at home.

Because I spent so much time there, I remember the living room well. The leather couch, stuffed chairs and console color T.V. crowded together in the middle of the room so that Mr. Schneider could display his hunting prowess around its periphery. Perched above a huge stone fireplace to the left and behind the T.V., an elk head crowned by a wide rack gazed down at us benevolently. On the floor in front of the fireplace, an open-mouthed bearskin rug bared its sharp teeth, and between the floor-to-ceiling windows on the right wall, a stuffed bobcat on a stand perpetually hissed. An owl attacking a mouse, a skinned rattlesnake, a snarling javelina, and a succession of mounted fish covered the walls.

Sunday afternoons at the Schneider house soon expanded into Saturdays as well, then after school on weekdays, and then all day every day during the summer. Mary, Deidre and I swam in the lake behind their house, played cowboys and Indians, climbed their two big cottonwood trees, and created make-believe dinners in their one-room playhouse. After these long days outside, Mrs. Schneider had us take off our shoes at the door. Then we giggled and squealed as we slid in our socks from one end of the family room to the other on the highly polished floor.

When I stayed overnight I shared Mary's double bed. Mary and I were the same age, on the verge of puberty. One evening when Mr. Schneider was gone, Mrs. Schneider unabashedly brought out biology books and, to my discomfort, explained to us the processes of menstruation and reproduction. She also advised us on how to take care of our skin in the dry Denver climate and washed our hair, one at a time, in the kitchen sink, rinsing it with vinegar to make it shine.

On those pleasant sleepovers, she taught us how to make streusel and then sat down at the dining room table with us while we ate it. Afterwards, she gathered the four of us beside her on the leather couch and told us stories in her soft, guttural German accent. Most of the stories were about wolves and castles and princesses and magic but once in a while she told us about the Holocaust and the other true terrors she escaped by leaving Germany at a young age.

When Mr. Schneider was gone on business or hunting trips, I sat in his place, at the head of the table. Dinner resembled the basic food groups we had learned at school: protein, starches, vegetables, and fruits. But at the Schneider house we ate the German version—a slice of sauerbraten or Weiner schnitzel, a scoop of potatoes, dumplings or spatzle, and a small pile of red cabbage or a green vegetable, with an Obsttorte (fruit torte) for dessert.

At my house, the whole family never ate dinner together, not even on Sundays. Instead, the children ate a chicken potpie, Hamburger Helper or some other frozen, canned or boxed meal, often in stages because everyone seemed to be on a different schedule. My father came home from work late, when most of us were either ready for bed or in bed. He then grilled steaks while my mother whipped up baked potatoes and a salad, and they ate together. On Friday and Saturday nights, they went out and found various older women to baby-sit us. Unless my father made his weekend orange juice, bacon, sausage, egg and toast brunch, our breakfasts, lunches, and snacks were make-your-own.

In the spring of my eleventh year, Mrs. Schneider took Mary, Deidre and me to an Easter party at her church. I wore one of Mary's new spring dresses and Mrs. Schneider wrapped my hair into a tight bun. There must have been a hundred women with their daughters, sitting in a big circle in the cathedral-ceiling Fellowship Hall, playing shower games and drinking tea out of china cups. I won a straw Easter hat rimmed with silk flowers that I kept for years and years.

The following summer Mrs. Schneider suddenly began coming over to my house. She sat at the kitchen table over coffee, earnestly talking to my mother while my young siblings ran up and down the stairs and in and out of the house, slamming doors, crying and pleading for attention. I cringed to see Mary, Deidre and Willie join them, scurrying between the piles of soiled clothes and toys and through air smacking of cat urine. Although Mrs. Schneider smiled at me, seemingly undisturbed by the dirt and commotion, I was embarrassed. And I didn't understand why, after she left, my mother went upstairs to her bedroom and came out later with red puffy eyes.

The next thing I knew, Mrs. Schneider was in the hospital. On the second day of her stay, my mother took Mary, Deidre and me to visit her. After greeting us with a wide smile, Mrs. Schneider talked with my mother about medical stuff. Not listening, Mary, Deidre and I gazed out the window at snowy Mount Evans, the brown foothills, and our rolling, tree-covered city. Finally, Mrs. Schneider's attention came back to us. As she asked about school and gave us homework advice, I could not help but notice that her bronzed skin had a yellow tinge to it and her short, straight brown hair was tangled and greasy.

She was only in the hospital for a week, and when she returned home, everything seemed to be about the same at the Schneider house. The only difference was that while I continued to spend most of my time at Mary and Deidre's house, Mrs. Schneider and Willie spent much of their time at mine.

In the fall, a few weeks after I had turned twelve, Mrs. Schneider was back in the hospital again. My mother took Mary, Deidre and me for visits; each successive visit she looked progressively thinner, paler and more tired. Her greasy hair fell out in clumps on the many pillows propping her up, her cheeks gradually sunk in and her face became spotted. As time passed, her soft voice became even softer, then it began shaking, and then she could not speak at all. She slept through our last few visits, shrunken under the sheet, with tubes coming out of her arms and nose. So many tubes. One day after school, my mother sat me down at the kitchen table and told me Mrs. Schneider had passed away. I bawled all night.

Her funeral was open-casket. The orange lipstick they painted on her lips was too bright and clashed with the rest of the make-up on her face. Scalp showed through her styled hair, her smile was tight and unnatural, her busy hands were forever clasped together. That was the last service I attended at the First Lutheran Church.

After Mrs. Schneider died, I could not spend much time at the Schneider's house. Mary tried to keep it as clean and orderly as her mother had but the atmosphere resonated with a silent anxiousness. Mr. Schneider seemed to be gone all the time and the stuffed animals haunted me. Their empty expressions mirrored the life that had vanished from this house.

My father then discovered an Episcopal Church with a youth program. Me and my oldest siblings, Mary, Deidre, and Willie went with him, and we soon became regular attendees. While we were gone, my mother prepared a lavish family dinner. This time, the Schneider family ate with us after church. Now it was our turn.

Peggy on Her 50th

By jd young

We started as sisters
Not our choice at birth
We grew as siblings
Quiet at first

I, dark and demanding
You, quiet and blonde
Gave in to adolescence
We spoke nary a word

Then came mid-life
With the husbands and kids
We grew too far apart
But - no need to forgive

Joy left our hearts
When the darkness appeared
We grew closer as friends
To fend off the fear

We can't pick our families
'Tho we prayed to that end
Now I'm blessed you're my sister
And - by choice - my friend

Piper Cub on an Alfalfa Field

By F. Clifton Berry, Jr.

Sometimes simple events of our childhood cause lifelong effects. Having shown a firm grasp of the obvious, let me mention two such events.

In the summer of 1941 I had turned 10 years old. Farming was a mainstay of the economy in North Central Illinois. Crops included corn, oats, hay, and soybeans, for example. Beef cattle and hogs complemented the crops and fed the slaughterhouses of the huge stockyards in Chicago, 90 miles to the east. Industry also provided jobs and income in our region. For example, the Westclox Company in our hometown of LaSalle-Peru was a major producer of watches and clocks. Fifty miles westward, the Boss Company in Kewanee produced superb work gloves.

One day in that summer, I was visiting Uncle Bert's farm outside the village of Neponset, a few miles east of Kewanee. He had just finished baling the most recent cutting of alfalfa from one of his hay fields. The last batch of bales lay stacked neatly on the hayrack, hitched to a green John Deere tractor for its trip to the barn. The hay baler machine, a Case machine also pulled by a John Deere tractor, stood silent near the gate to the barnyard.

Uncle Bert and his helpers had been explaining the baling process to us kids. In the next year and throughout the war years, I was one of those helpers every summer. For now, I was the inquisitive kid.

The tractors were quiet. The distinctive alfalfa aroma wafted in the warm air. We stood on the stubble and talked. The afternoon quiet was soon broken by the pop-pop of an engine that grew louder fairly fast. No vehicles moved along the gravel road. We looked upward, and there was an airplane headed our way.

An airplane!

We knew about airplanes, of course. We had read about them, seen them in the movies, but had no experience with them.

The bright yellow airplane approached and flew right above us, probably at about 1,000 feet altitude. It made a wide circle at that height, and then began to descend, pointed right at Uncle Bert's alfalfa field. He knew it was coming, but we boys didn't.

The engine noise diminished as the yellow airplane descended. Its wings wiggled a bit as it approached the newly-mown field, then its wheels touched, and it rolled along toward us, slowing as it neared. We had read about the Piper Cub, and now one of them was right in front of us.

The airplane stopped, the engine stopped, and the propeller did likewise. Someone inside the little airplane lifted the side door upward and climbed out, followed by the other occupant. It was Uncles LeRoy and Paul, my dad's and Uncle Bert's younger brothers.

One of them thanked Uncle Bert for the use of his field as a landing strip. They asked if we'd like to look at the airplane. Would we? Yes, indeed.

The uncles walked us around the Cub, pointing out its essential components, and warning us to stay well away from the wooden two-blade propeller. An occasional click came from the engine as it cooled. Otherwise all was quiet, save for the voices and our occasional "Wow."

Uncle LeRoy asked me if I wanted to sit in the airplane. Yes, indeed, again. He showed me how to climb in correctly and sit in the front seat. The Cub of 1941 did not have a crowded instrument panel, but it was certainly impressive to me. The distinctive scent of an airplane cabin was present. This was a much different machine from the cars, trucks, and tractors we knew.

Dismounting, I rejoined the uncles as they conversed. The big question was, why did they have the airplane? The answer made sense. Both uncles were soldiers in the Illinois National Guard, the 33d Infantry Division. That summer of 1941, the 33d and many other National Guard and active

Army units were participating in maneuvers as part of the preparation for war.

The Tennessee Maneuvers were held over many weeks in the countryside around Camp Forrest near Tullahoma, northwest of Chattanooga. Camp Forrest lay almost 600 miles away from the uncles' home in Neponset. They decided to buy the airplane, learn to fly and use it for the back and forth trips to Camp Forrest. "Wow" again.

After a bit, it was time for them to go. They picked up some fragments of dried alfalfa and threw them into the air to determine the wind direction. Uncle Paul climbed into the pilot's seat. Uncle LeRoy put both hands on the propeller. Soon Uncle Paul yelled, "Contact." Uncle LeRoy pulled down briskly on the propeller, and stepped back. The engine coughed, then roared to life, the propeller transformed from a slab of wood to a shimmering circle at the Cub's nose.

Uncle LeRoy climbed into the back seat, shut the door, and the Cub began to taxi across the field. Its nose swung into the wind, the engine roared, and the Cub rolled across the field and climbed into the sky. Uncle Bert said they were headed to Kewanee, where they kept the Cub at the airfield not far from the National Guard Armory.

The Cub's engine noise faded. The field was quiet. The bales of alfalfa waited to be stowed in the barn. We turned to, following Uncle Bert's directions on doing it right.

From that moment, I wanted to fly.

The Tennessee Maneuvers of 1941 helped the U.S. Army prepare for war. The war came within a few months, with the Japanese attack on Pearl Harbor. Uncles LeRoy and Paul and millions of other young men soon went to war. Before they shipped out, Grandma and Grandpa Berry let the Cub be stored in their garage, with wings removed, for the duration.

Whenever we visited Grandma and Grandpa, they let me sit in the Cub. I wanted to learn more about airplanes. Soon I bought my first airplane model kit. It was a Piper Cub with fuselage made of balsa wood, covered with tissue paper and its propeller powered by a rubber band.

Uncles LeRoy and Paul returned at war's end. They sold the Piper Cub and returned to civilian pursuits.

My interest in flying intensified during the war and after. Upon graduation from high school, I immediately joined the U.S. Air Force to be around airplanes. I wasn't a pilot, but served in an aircraft control and warning group on the Berlin Airlift.

A few years later, in the 82d Airborne Division I learned to jump out of perfectly good airplanes in flight. Finally, after more years I learned to fly, first with six hours on the Piper Cub and then into soloing the Cessna 172 and continuing to fly into my mid-Seventies.

That childhood afternoon on the alfalfa field motivated me for life.

The Power of Peaches and Petunias

By Karen Brown

On summer evenings I smell my petunias, those earthy, musky flowers that remind me of her, and ache for her to come back and be my grandma again. I stayed with her often. When I was little, a week's visit at her house in town was part of my summer vacation. We worked in her garden during the day, then after supper we sat under the shade trees drinking iced tea out of Mason jars, watching the long summer evenings fade into night.

If pressed to remember what we talked about, I could not say. But we passed the time in pleasant contemplation, noting the comings and goings of neighbors, the sights and sounds of a small town settling down for the night. If we planned to wash windows the next day, I knew that she would call a neighbor and ask to borrow her stepladder and that I would be sent to fetch it and take it back when we were finished.

Sunday mornings and some Wednesday evenings Grandma went to church, often wearing a lacy lavender blouse and plaid skirt. I thought she looked especially pretty in lavender–and years later I discovered that my coloring, too, found lavender complimentary. I liked that, and the fact that I favored, physically and emotionally, her side of the family.

In those days of no television and poor radio reception people, especially relatives, found entertainment in visiting each other. Normally, I squirmed and fidgeted through visits with adult relatives. My tomboy instincts wanted me outside pretending to be Black Beauty or Trigger, but Daddy had some notion that sitting in a room filled with our soporific relatives would make a young lady of me. Some of these relatives appeared to me to be at once victims of, and enforcers for, their church and the Bible. Their gloomy interpretations of God's laws and wrath sucked the joy from not only their own lives but from mine and, I suspect, everyone who had to listen to them.

Grandma, however, was different. Her quiet love of life and people calmed and soothed me like a glass of warm milk at bedtime. Hidden behind her Mona Lisa grin and that playful twinkle in her eyes lay a life lived in harsh times, in a harsh country–the Oklahoma panhandle during the Great Depression and Dust Bowl days. But she was too stubborn to let her troubles show, and too tough to whine about God's laws and wrath.

Once, when I was about eleven, I spent most of the summer helping her with housework and gardening while she recovered from surgery. I never knew what kind of surgery. Adults of that era told children what they thought they should know, and everything else was none of their business. If I had asked about the surgery I knew the answer would be: "Don't ask so many questions."

I resented, not that I had to go help Grandma, but that almost all of my summer vacation would be eaten away in isolation from the farm, from my family and friends, from wading in puddles after it rained, from swimming in the cow tank, from flirting with the boys in my Sunday School class. I didn't know anyone in town; no kids my age lived nearby–except for one boy who must have had friends of his own to play with. He never came to get acquainted, and I was too shy to go talk to him.

But someone had to spend the summer with Grandma, and since I was next to the youngest of five children–too young to drive a tractor and couldn't milk a cow—was expendable. And my slow, dreamy approach to labor put me less in demand than my older siblings. So I packed my Levi's and T-shirts and resigned myself to a summer of solitary confinement.

I missed my family and dog Laddie, with that silly game he played bringing me dirt clods to throw so he could chase them and bring them back, slimy with slobbers, for me to throw again. And I missed the farm and its country noises–tractors chugging, mockingbirds singing, cows mooing, the windmill pumping outside my bedroom window the exquisite solitude when everyone was gone but me. But in town the birds still sang, and I learned to enjoy other sounds, the train's whistle, the siren that announced the arrival of lunchtime at noon every day, the swish of cars driving by the house, Grandma's soap operas on the radio.

Grandma always raised a garden, always planted petunias. As she grew older, arthritis slowed her down but couldn't stop her from growing her garden. She called her aches and pains the "rheumatiz" and rubbed horse liniment on her knees every night. When that pungent smell drifted into my bedroom I knew she would soon be slipping into her nightgown, scrubbing her false teeth, and saying goodnight.

She went up and down stairs sideways, like a two-year-old child, holding onto the rail with both hands–four steps down to get to the garden and four steps up to get back to the kitchen. She kept her gardening shoes just inside the back door, near the steps, and slipped into them every morning on her way to the garden. She was proud that she had trimmed down from over 300 pounds to just 165, but her heart still suffered from having hauled the extra weight around for so long. She puffed, struggling up and down those stairs, emitting a little groan or "whooeee" when she reached the top or bottom. I walked behind her, always hoping she wouldn't fall, always a little astonished at her perseverance and determination.

In the mornings, before the sun was high and scorching, I moved the hose and sprinkler around to water the grass and the garden. I hoed the weeds between the rows of green beans, snap peas, and little yellow pear tomatoes. I trimmed the edges of the garden so the Bermuda grass wouldn't take over. Grandma and I picked grapes and plums, and I climbed the peach tree to pick the biggest, plumpest peaches I ever saw, before or since. She stood at the bottom of the tree and guided me from peach to peach. "Right over here, just to your left. No, back a little bit. . .right there." I dropped them into her outstretched apron and she piled them in her bucket.

After a morning of picking fruit, we sat at the kitchen table and seeded purple grapes for jelly until our fingers looked like we had been playing in an inkwell. We pitted the plums and peaches for Grandma's freezer and fresh cobblers, the most awesome cobblers ever to come out of an oven. She made the dough with Bisquick, marbling it through the fruit, creating a work of art with just the right mixture of fruit and dough. The kitchen, the entire small house shimmered with a fragrant glow while the cobbler baked. Then we scooped vanilla ice cream over it, warm from the oven, and ate until Grandma pushed her dish back and said, with a naughty little grin, "I shouldn't have et so much."

Years later, when I lived far away, homesick for a taste of my childhood and my favorite relative, I wrote asking her for her cobbler recipe. She sent it to me on the back of a tiny envelope with a fancy scalloped flap, written in her choppy handwriting, her old fashioned, undereducated way with words:

Cobbler

1 ½ Bisquick make thin batter pour in well greace pan fix your fruit suger it good put oils in some spice in peach or apple but cherry almond flavor but I expect you have other kind fruit down there cimmon and nutmeg spices that kind use

I followed her guesswork recipe the best I could, mentally drooling as the cobbler baked, taking myself back to Grandma's kitchen and simpler, cozier days. As I finally pulled my cobbler out of the oven, however, I faced my first cooking calamity. My cobbler bore no resemblance to Grandma's. It didn't even smell like Grandma's. It just lay there in the pan with its store-bought peaches and flat, sloppy dough, breaking my heart. I can't remember if it was edible. Chances are I was too disappointed to taste it.

I never tried to make Grandma's cobbler again, though I still have that precious recipe fifty years later. Grandma was and always will be the cobbler queen. No one, especially not I, can ever match her skill with fruit and Bisquick.

But every spring I plant pots and pots of petunias to set on my deck rail where I can sniff their warm perfume as I water them. I love their many different colors—red, white, pink, purple, lavender—though the darkest ones give off the richest scents. A petunia's beauty is in its elegant simplicity; it thrives under adverse conditions; it is tough and hardy. Like Grandma. Petunias don't require any special skill to grow. The only hard part is that, like the peach cobbler, the main ingredient is . . . no longer here.

At Grandma's funeral someone pulled me away from her coffin. I had grabbed its sides, sobbing, longing to touch her warm, liver-spotted hands, the hands that planted petunias and baked peach cobbler, yet not touching them because I knew they would be cold and hard with embalming fluid.

I never knew who pulled me away. Whoever it was probably thought he was doing me a kindness, sparing me a bit of grief. But it didn't feel like kindness. It felt like being disciplined, like a naughty child caught making rude noises in church. What, I wondered was so bad about crying at her coffin, about letting go of the grief I felt? Was I embarrassing someone? Were they afraid I would start screaming, make a spectacle of myself? And what if I did? People in other cultures, of other religions grieve openly, wailing and screaming, letting go of their pain. In our culture we hold it in, stifling our emotions.

I wonder what would have happened if that someone had not dragged me away from Grandma's coffin, forced me to cover up my pain. Perhaps I would have embarrassed not only myself, but my entire family. Grandma herself probably would not have approved of my losing my dignity in that way, but she would have understood. And I would not have walked away from her funeral feeling cheated of my last chance to say good-bye to her, to her kind and generous spirit, to her cobbler and her garden. Still, that experience confirmed for me something I often suspected was true–that I had always been inexplicably out of sync with all of my relatives but Grandma.

The Recital

By Frederick Dove

"No, no, *no,*" said Mr. Biddleman, his voice rising with each repetition. "I said staccato and fortissimo. It's an Indian war dance. If you goof it won't sound any better played softly. Once more from the top. Ignore mistakes and keep the rhythm going."

His words still ringing in the dusty air, I took a deep breath and resolved to face my fate like a man. Squares of light from the dingy window behind me tumbled unevenly across the gloomy little rehearsal room, barely illuminating the brand new music book perched on the ancient piano. I took some small comfort in the fact that at this time on a Saturday morning there would be no one else in the church to witness my disgraceful display. No one except my older sister, Pat, waiting just outside the door. Her lesson had gone flawlessly as usual.

Again I plunged into the *Tomahawk Dance,* both hands pumping the two-fingered chords with renewed energy. I cringed with each wrong note but plowed on in an effort to keep the ponderous beat moving. Even though I hated playing the piano, ironically, I was anxious to move on to something more challenging. *Tomahawk Dance* was basically *Chopsticks* with a native Indian twist. To screw it up was truly humiliating, even for an eight-year-old.

Just four bars from the end, my spirits began to rise, only to come crashing down once again when Biddleman suddenly yelled, "Enough, enough," waving his arms as if swatting at flies. His expression suggested there might be a foul odor in the room. "Go home and practice," he said. "Don't come back again next week unless you can play this song. The recital is a week after that and I will not have you make a fool out of both of us."

Without a word, I closed my music book and slid off the bench.

"Take some pointers from your sister," he added when I reached the doorway. I kept walking.

Outside, leaves covered the main street like colorful litter from the Mummers Day parade. I filled my nose with the musty smell of them and headed toward the bus stop five blocks away. Pat's legs were longer than mine, but I held my lead. I had had enough for one day and was in no mood for any comments from her.

The three and four-story red brick buildings that looked down on us in the center of town were all drearily similar except for the small signs out front that identified them as a diner, a shoe store, a florist or a clothing store. Only the movie theater broke the monotonous mold with its jutting marquee sheathed in lights and box office festooned with garish posters.

A block from the town square, I paused at Bean's Novelty Shop. Corny practical jokes with clever names like *Fake Bird's Hit* and *Wind-up Joy Buzzer* lined the wide display windows out front. Inside, superheroes doing heroic things leapt off the covers of row upon row of action comic books. It was my favorite store, the only place in town where you could find such indispensable items as snap snot, plastic vomit, and sticks of phony chewing gum that delivered a shock when tugged on. I loved the idea of people playing jokes on each other just for the sheer fun of it, and I liked nothing better than to explore the place when time permitted, imagining the fun I could have with each silly novelty. The store was chock-full of so many items dumped so haphazardly into so many bins that I couldn't even imagine how many days it would take to sort through it all. But there was no time to go in and look around, let alone buy anything before the bus arrived. Besides, I had no money.

After dinner, I went to the den and banged on the piano some more, serving my nightly sentence of thirty minutes hard labor on *Tomahawk Dance*. The sounds of my two best friends, Eric and Timmy, playing Catch in the warm autumn

100

air outside fueled my resentment to near breaking point. I kept my eyes on the music book while a metronome and a wind-up timer ticked away together on top of the piano.

With the prospect of having to play the piece in front of a crowd looming ever closer, I was trying my best, but to my growing annoyance, I kept making the same mistake at a point where I had to reach up and turn the page. Exasperated, I stubbornly played the passage again, finally flipping the page at just the right instant. A tantalizing breeze rustled the filmy curtains and flipped the page back again. I grabbed the book, threw it on the floor and began stomping on it.

My mother entered the room, walking fast, jaw set, and stopped a foot away. "Is this what you call practicing? You're supposed to practice the music, not the actual war dance." She pinned me with a stern stare long enough for her words to sink in, then added, "Wait right here."

I heard her say something to my father in the kitchen while I meekly replaced the book on the music rack, resigned to whatever came next. She returned with a tall glass of iced tea and placed it next to the timer, which she reset for an hour. I opened my mouth to protest, but her expression left no doubt that it would not be wise. Outside, Eric and Timmy stopped to watch when my mother took a seat next to me on the piano bench. They were too far away to hear our words, but with uncanny certainty they read our gestures and expressions and fell on the ground laughing.

My mother glanced at me impatiently. "Let's get started," she said.

My face burned with humiliation, but I kept my mouth shut and started once again to pound on the obnoxious chords, knowing that this was to be a familiar drill from now until the dreaded recital.

"Yes, that's it," Mr. Biddleman cried, slapping his hands on the edge of the piano like an Indian brave beating a tom-tom. "Much better. Keep going. I feel the rhythm now."

Encouraged, I hit the keys a little harder, happy just to avoid another browbeating. As I approached the final stanza, he said, "Don't stop. One more time. Keep the rhythm going," and began clapping his hands and stomping his foot on the frayed carpet as if I were performing at a square dance and he had lucked out with a front row seat.

Obediently, I started once more from the top, concentrating on the notes, turning the page at just the right time, and finessing the mistakes by plowing ahead like a trooper. Biddleman clapped and stomped approvingly, nodding his head, no doubt secretly validating his own incredible teaching abilities.

When I finished he said, "Well done. There is hope for you yet." He smiled and I was a bit moved by his show of sincerity. Then he spoiled it by adding, "You must be learning from your sister."

My dad squeezed the Cadillac into the closest space that he could find to the Hagerstown Museum of Fine Art. The thick pillars and concrete dome loomed high above stone bridges and narrow streams meandering to the man-made lake of the city park. My mother and sister checked their makeup in the rear-view mirror one last time before opening their doors. We shuffled through the fragrant leaves without speaking.

Inside the main viewing room, people were milling about, chatting quietly and occasionally fanning themselves with the bulletins. Imposing figures stared down from enormous paintings that climbed more than twenty feet up all four walls. Folding metal chairs covered the expanse of gleaming hardwood floor, and at the front of the room, an old mahogany piano squatted forlornly.

I followed my parents into the room with a mixture of excitement and apprehension. My father stopped at a row near the front and gestured for my mom to slide in. "You two are the performers tonight, so we'll give you the aisle seats," he said and slid in next to my mom. Ever the gentleman, I gestured for my sister to go first. But she wanted the outside seat, so I shrugged and took the seat next to my dad.

My thoughts were totally on my performance, which had taken on new significance when my father promised us five dollars each if we played without a mistake. Unlike my sister, this was my first recital and I was anxious to get it over with. Then again, I was determined to do it right because five dollars was a lot of money. I was nervous enough that I had to perform the song in front of so many people without the added pressure of having to do it perfectly. I consoled myself with the knowledge that no matter what happened, tonight's events would put an end to the pain and misery that I had suffered for these seemingly countless weeks.

The overhead lights dimmed and footlights appeared under the lonely piano. The chatter of the crowd dropped to a low murmur. I glanced at the bulletin and felt a pang of horror race down my body like a lightning bolt down a tree. The performers were listed in alphabetical order and the very first name was mine. *Why hadn't someone warned me?* I felt angry and betrayed. Somehow I had assumed that we would go in order of age or skill or years of experience. Anything but this.

Mr. Biddleman walked to the piano. I watched, stricken, as he welcomed the crowd and rambled on about his piano school. A sense of foreboding began to overtake me, draining all the energy from my body, leaving behind a limp and vacuous facade. Like a dream where something bad is about to happen and you can't stop it, I heard my name spoken and the crowd began to applaud politely. My sister made way for me, a callous grin appearing at the sight of my pallid face.

"Go ahead," my father whispered.

I stepped into the aisle and walked to the piano on spongy legs. My mouth was dry and my heart was pounding as I seated myself on the hard wooden bench, too nervous to look toward the crowd. Instead, I stared straight ahead at the empty music rack, the prospect of playing the whole song from memory now ludicrous and insane. With difficulty I swallowed and placed my clammy fingers on the keys. The slightest pressure would sound the first note and then there was no turning back. My performance had to be flawless. My five dollars hung in the balance.

I breathed deeply, once, twice, acutely aware of the murmuring and rustling of the crowd. Another second's pause and I plunged in, praying that my sweaty fingers wouldn't slip off the keys. As soon as I began hammering the familiar chords, I felt an odd sense of déjà vu, a comforting feeling that the loathsome tune was now ingrained in my psyche, so deeply programmed that nothing could stop me. With growing confidence, I banged away on the discordant chords, feeling invincible. On the verge of arrogance, my hand involuntarily snapped up at the point where I had been turning the page.

The crowd took it as a display of showmanship and responded with muted applause. At that point, one of my fingers slid off the key and pinched the one next to it, sounding a strident clunker. Mortified, I plunged on without missing a beat, a slave to the relentless training I had been forced to endure. In my mind's eye the five dollar bill was flying away on tiny wings, even as the morbid realization that what's done is done gave me new resolve. I pounded the keys harder, so sick of the trivial song that I was caught between a sensation of physical illness and an emotional fatigue so deep it numbed all other senses.

Then I stopped. My hands seemed to realize before my brain that the song was over. I slowly pulled my fingers from the keys, and emboldened by enormous relief, finally turned to face the crowd. Steadier now, I rose from the bench and bowed. The applause seemed unusually loud, the smiles unexpected. In a daze of fading adrenaline, I walked triumphantly back down the aisle to my family.

Behind me, Mr. Biddleman took the stage, thanked me and introduced my sister. Ignoring my smirk, she brushed past me and headed to the front. My father offered his hand as I reclaimed the seat next to him. I shook it. He held my hand an instant longer then placed four dollars in it. I must have looked bewildered. "One mistake is one dollar," he said. I nodded, too drained to think of a reply.

I looked away and closed my fist tightly around the crisp bills. I had thought I lost the whole five dollars, just assuming that it was all or nothing. But I was starting to learn that few things in life are that absolute. As my sister began her sonata with precision and feeling, it occurred to me that it was a good thing that no one had told me that each mistake was worth a dollar. Sometimes it's better not to know. After the first mistake, only the conviction that I had already blown it and lost all the money allowed me to relax and play as well as I had. If it hadn't been for that, I wouldn't have had four whole dollars to spend at Bean's Novelty Shop after my next piano lesson.

A School on a Mountain

By Catharine Cool

Arriving in Malaya for my first Christmas vacation from an Australian boarding school, I tried to tell my mother how much I dreaded returning to *Woodroyd*. But even at seven she could freeze my tears with ridicule.

"Come now, my dear, you're far too big to cry," she'd say at the end of any outburst. And since I was so tall for my age, it seemed a double rebuke.

Though Charlotte was also on vacation from the government school where she was teaching, her added social life left me spending much time with my Chinese amah and when I did get to be with my mother, I was so thrilled at everything she offered, I chose to forget what I knew was inevitable - I'd have to go back.

Luckily my childish distress was re-enforced by reports from my grandmother - *You must get Catharine out of the Woodroyd School. Every time I take her back, (which I regret is not very often), she cries and cries. A child should not have to resort to tears like that!*

Finally convinced, Charlotte decided to move me to another boarding school.

"You'll love the new school we've chosen for you," she announced just before the end of the holidays. "It's up in the hills with such a lovely big garden to play in – even ponies to ride on!"

The thought of ponies and an escape from the unpleasant confines of *Woodroyd*, pleased me immensely.

But first there was another long boat trip on my own.

Lying in the cabin I looked out the porthole, imagining some terrible but welcome storm causing the ship to be wrecked, but with all the passengers – or certainly the children aboard - successfully rescued! Surely they'd have to return me to my parents in Kota Bahru, Malaya to recover for at least a year? Or maybe I'd be drowned and then how sorry my parents would be!

But alas, the voyage was smooth and the stewardess in charge of small children was kind and wary, leaving no chance for one to fall overboard and be thrillingly rescued and then pampered.

Over the years since the "school ships" began to carry child passengers, the crew of Blue Funnel steamships had become expert in handling wild, colonial offspring shuffled between parents and boarding schools each Christmas vacation. I'm sure many of us smaller returnees on the return trip were quite easy to control - distressed and homesick as we were at how many weeks and months now lay ahead before the next Christmas with parents. But the adolescents I think caused quite a little havoc and the crew must have sighed with relief at every journey's end.

I can still lovingly recall the Captain, another dear, goat-teed gentleman (my obvious preference in those days). I remember his making a fuss of me throughout the voyage, and hugging me close at the farewell party – but I knew in my heart, it was a played-out role, the pleasure transitory. At the homeport of Fremantle we'd all be off-loaded and sent back to the dreaded prisons of boarding school again.

Despite living and working in Malaya, Charlotte had kept in close touch with her friend Mary who'd been at Perth Modern School as well as at Teacher's Training School with her. Both had strong views on innovative education. Over the years Mary had highly recommended a boarding school called *Stawell* poised near the summit of Mt Lofty in the hills above Adelaide, the capital city of South Australia where Mary lived. Pushed for a quick decision, Charlotte decided to follow this suggestion, so it was to there I was dispatched on my return to Australia.

Stawell was set in a landscape of gardens and bush-land. The school emblem depicted a little holly tree clipped to the shape of an umbrella and covered with red berries. The tree, which was the model for this, grew in the center of a small maze in front of the school; a mansion which looked out over the foothills running down to the plains. The mansion was used for the boarding school and beyond the main garden, another large building served as the classrooms. There were some 40 students, of whom only 12 were boarders. At seven, I was among the three youngest boarders. The other two were sisters whose mother was part owner of the school. Since most of the other boarders were teenagers, we three "littlies" were allowed special freedoms.

It was a remarkable school, run by a wise and endearing woman – Mabel Phyllis Hardy. She allowed students to pursue their studies as far and as deeply in any subject as they wished. By the end of the first year, I was studying Latin and French and Botany; the literature of Blake and Dickens, World History from Van Loon, classical Ballet with Nora Stewart, (who had trained the famous Robert Helpman) and music with the nuns from a nearby convent. We wrote our own poetry, composed music, carried out real laboratory experiments and had classics such as *"Great Expectations"* read to us each night - with cocoa by the fire in the headmistress' living room.

But those pleasures did not come easily or soon.

Returning to any boarding school after the joyous freedom of the Christmas vacation spent with my parents in a real house without rules, prefects or school bells, was difficult. At home, with the brief imperative of Christmas spirit and school vacation, I was a special person, a daughter and an only child.

In *Woodroyd*, I'd been only one of many ordinary students, with most of us stoically enduring the unhappiness of being held captive in boarding school. How could I foretell that *Stawell* might be different?

I remember so many summer nights when I was seven, shut into the dormitory at eight-fifteen; the hot, thick sky still poking yellow fingers through the blinds. I'd lie twisting and fretting on the jailer sheets, until sleep's white fist knocked me down a tunnel of escape. Blue seemed the only color that cared for me, against the empty windows, bringing morning. Although I came to love being at *Stawell,* those first months were lonely and unnerving.

It was dark in the dormitory; the six tall windows always hugely full of black sky. I huddled in my bed, second from the windows. So many shadows between the door and my bed; so much to be frightened of, even though two other children were in the dormitory with me. I was told that seven was too old to be afraid of the dark, but I was. So much space hovered within the dorm and all around the twenty-roomed mansion and the acres of garden. The dorm held four beds and each bed had its own chest of drawers against the wall. Everything seemed enormous.

Across the large bay window was a padded seat on which we, (the three youngest boarders) would often kneel to gaze out at the gardens. The gardens were exceptional filled with huge rhododendrons, azaleas of every color; lilacs, camellias and hundreds of specimens of exotic shrubs and trees. I remember there were three dormitories for the dozen boarders, plus a dining room and the headmistress's suite, the infirmary upstairs and the great lounge downstairs in which "visiting parents" met their children.

For those who have never experienced being sent away to boarding school, it is hard to explain the overwhelming feeling of loss. With even the brief security of family life stripped away, I felt left with no identity. I belonged to no one. I was a name and could occupy space only if I conformed to the dictates of the school structure that held me. As I grew older, I learned to play the game; I built my own shelters, but at first it was frightening for I was very shy.

Long afternoons later I wrote -

Why did they send us all away
Forsaken children, cargo-ed across
To the underground of boarding school;
Our rock-a-bye skins salted in tears.

I still find it difficult to write about those early months

at boarding school-left wondering what it does to small children to tear them from their families and send them off to schools far away. Too young to comprehend the "Why?" they just have to wordlessly accept the change.

In the green garden of that school, perhaps the long afternoons still nurse on the soft-bosomed clouds swelling around Mt. Lofty. If I went back, would I find where the anxiety began? In the garden? In the wet shrubs by the window or in the tall trees sighing beyond the dormitory walls? So dark were those nights, so full of whispers of love withdrawn.

To my frightened seven-year-old self it wasn't just the garden at night that scared me. By day it was the immense wilderness of scrub and trees that flowed from the edge of the gardens over all the hills and swooped down to the faraway sea. There was no safe place to hide from the strangeness of this new school and its surroundings.

After the close, wet tropics - to be exposed to this vast scrubland was disturbing. At Woodroyd Street with its small, dark rooms and confinement, I'd not felt threatened like this. My Western Australian parents growing up in rural and semi-rural settings carved out at the edge of bush and desert might have been accustomed to this kind of unbounded psychic space. I was not.

One day, when I was hanging back from the group of boarders walking to Sunday school through the edge of bushland we had to cross to get to church, Miss Hardy, the headmistress, came up to me saying, "What strange things are growing here. See these plants? They look like grass trees with tall sticks in their middle. I used to be scared of them when I was little like you. They're called *Black Boys* and they're very old, their trunks blackened by past bushfires. They grow in funny groups like families walking through the scrub - like us walking to Sunday school. Come and touch this spike, it's like a wand of flowers."

I was entranced; I walked up and touched. It felt surprisingly soft and the grass-tufted mounds that supported them seemed like skirts. Indeed they did resemble stick

110

people. My fear evaporated as I held Miss Hardy's hand. She radiated her love of the curious shrubs and trees we walked amongst. Odd-ness could be lovable and friendly it seemed. I wanted to believe that. In the warm sun and with her closeness, it was possible.

Later when I discovered little Virginia Howard was also scared of the bush, I made my first friend by reassuring her there was nothing to be afraid of. "Trees and plants are really another form of people!" I gravely assured her.

So as the year drew on through winter into spring, I began to feel I belonged. Safe in the new triumvirate of the two Howard sisters and myself, I discovered school could be exciting and interesting. The teachers at *Stawell* were warm and sensitive to what we children were thinking. We had status, we were important.

The assembly room at *Stawell* was walled in glass and trees – with no seeming separation between the two. Every morning we stood against the far wall of the huge room singing hymns. Waist-high to the Prefects, I murmured the half understood words with serious delight. John Buchan's ghosts "sent up" from *Pilgrim's Progress* read before each morning assembly also swirled in the sunlit fluidity of glass and trees. To the little girl I was, God seemed so plural, so powerful - the three in one became muddled with gods of the seas, gods of the earth, gods of the air. I felt the visual spirits flowing round the heavens as I sang and sang.

The schoolrooms at *Stawell* were built into the hillside flanks of Mt Lofty. From the windows you looked into space and treetops. Inside, you felt as if you were in the trees themselves.

Behind the assembly room, branches of small rooms fanned back towards the hill's flank. There was a sensation of being suspended, of being "en plein air," all that glass to let in sun and then the fall to the valleys below to suffuse one with light.

Miss Hardy and the other teachers conducted classes informally as though they were seminars. I recall no desks, no rows of 'attentioned' children - just listening and growing our fantasies under the spell of innovative and dedicated teaching.

Miss Hardy offered so much to us – opening many doors to other people's secret gardens through ideas revealed in words and music. Many of these ideas revealed emotions of awe and the need to idolize, to respect and admire – to move outside oneself to be either that heroine or hero or, perhaps better still, to be the "pleasured spectator." This is where I believe the real trigger to creativity resides. This need to expand a desire to make one's own pleasure - to learn to tend it and weed out what cannot develop further.

So many nights in her small room beside a wood fire before bedtime, Miss Hardy read aloud to us three special boarders about other people's mind-adventures and we took these ideas back to our dormitory beds and they grew and were accepted into our own fertile thought-fields of childhood. Today, with TV and movies doing that in another form perhaps this sounds rather primitive – and yet just think how it helped the imagination of our young flexible minds create our OWN pictures for the stories, not someone else's - and therein lies the enormous difference. We were offered not gathered facts lined up in textbooks, but whole unbounded visions of other times and cultures and these we could adapt and cut to our own design.

One book I vividly remember was written by John Masefield and titled *Dauber*. It told of a sailor who painted – this intrigued me immensely and I spent hours in bed at night in the dormitory imagining him capturing the color and excitement of the sea on a page of paper.

At *Stawell*, safe in our kingdom on that mountain top, we could indulge our own fantasies. True we were bereft of family – but this other world was retribution of a sort.

The breadth of what Miss Hardy offered our minds from the ages of 7-10, was unusual. We had no set textbooks, the quick drift and overlap from literature to science, art and even other religions was so essential a part of the mind-set she gave. Van Loon's *Approach to History and Civilization* was the nearest she came to using a textbook.

During my first year at *Stawell* my mother didn't write letters to me very often, but on one occasion she sent me a set of postcards of the Sultan of Kelantan's Coronation – pictures of bedecked floats of carved jeweled animals carried by slaves, of robed courtiers standing beside a crowned Sultan, of rows of cheering subjects lining the road.

To my two friends and I living on our distant mountain in Australia, it proved that real kings existed and strange idols for different gods were still carried shoulder-high amongst applauding heathen hordes.

Poring over those postcards in our boarding school dormitory, we spent hours nodding to each other in satisfied awe.

I still have those postcards.

In my last years at *Stawell* we had become fast friends with Nancy, the school cook. Plump and motherly she was well aware that we mounted raids on the kitchen after hours when the older students were still studying before bedtime.

Into the darkened kitchen we would creep to assemble a sort of confection – for we seldom were allowed candy or "lollies" (as we called them) but sometimes the craving for a substitute led us kitchen-wards where we made up our own concoction of Golden Syrup, raisins and shredded coconut. This we scrambled together and consumed with much delight, remembering Nancy's quiet counsel – "only take the little basins and leave no mess on the counter. I'll cover for you!"

We loved her. She knew of our crime – her knowing and still allowing it, was the added essence. Here was a real accomplice and we adored her loyalty.

On one occasion Nancy was even allowed to take us to the beach. Quite an expedition, so I remember it well.

A trip on the bus – for just us Nancy and the three of us, traveling all the way down to the city of Adelaide – then on a tram to the beach at GLENELG. (We were especially taken with the idea that *glenelg* was the same spelt backwards as forwards).

As the tram trundled along its rails we twittered quietly to ourselves with our "adventure". This was even better than going with a regular adult – this was with a special adult "friend."

Glenelg was my first real Australian beach – it lies there so tranquil in memory. The sea is dead calm – I can walk right into it and not drown – there are no unsettling waves to be sucked into– just the quiet, blue water.

I can touch it - it is passive and soft, shallow and gently curling under my toes.

"Come on," says my friend Lucinda and we tiptoe into the sea.

Here was no nightmare of drowning. Here was a new dream to replace it – a friend's hand to hold and the sun's warm touch of reassurance on one's shoulder.

There on the huge yellow sand-fields we lay and played for hours – rushing in to splash in the shallows and out again - doing just what we wanted while Nancy lazed watchfully on the beach. It was heavenly – a full release from the prison of school – we were finally like the other children who laughed nearby with their parents.

Poor Nancy had a hard time getting us to leave the beach but we knew it was a long bus ride back and we had no desire to get her into trouble, so we reluctantly obeyed.

However Nancy did end up being roundly chastised, for in the following days it was evident that all three of us children were badly sunburned. Indeed in the following week we were all quite sick from the burning of our mountain-sheltered skins and the dormitory became a house of moans. Poor red-haired Lucinda with her very fair skin ended up wrapped in towels soaked in yellow picric acid and eventually shed what seemed her whole upper torso's skin.

This, her sister and I helped pull off in macabre delight.

Later, when we heard our loved Nancy had been

severely reprimanded we trailed in to Miss Hardy with incensed complaints.

In her usual gentle way Miss Hardy listened carefully and added – "I am glad you wish to protect your friend, but she ought to have known better and now you also know - that's the good thing isn't it? The sun and the sea are not just pleasurable, they have power as well as beauty – respect them - for like the earth and the world they are not ours and they can certainly harm those who do not respect them."

We trailed away solemnly nodding in satisfied understanding.

I find I can recall her every word.

Stawell School raised much of its own fruit - apples, peaches and plums. It even had its own strawberry and gooseberry patch, quite a large area under wire mesh usually padlocked against a group of student thieves. Of which, I must confess, my two friends and I were such. Indeed we were only finally caught after several successful forays.

On that particular day the sun beamed warmly generous, the sky was brightest blue and the fat, hot berries grinned from the dark green leaves. On and on, we moved down the rows out of the sheltered corner and nearer to the kitchen. Besotted with strawberries and giggles, we became careless, and then over the wire mesh, the heavy-bosomed wrath of a Prefect boomed. Pamela Frank had seen us! Trapped like rabbits in a hutch, we skittered up and down the wire, scared but thrilled at the chase. The Prefect's bulk finally darkened the gate; in cowed surrender we emerged to be led to the principal.

In a line we stood, aged seven, eight and nine. What would be done with us? The headmistress scowled at the Prefect to depart. We quailed.

"Well!" said Miss Hardy, Miss Mabel Phyllis Hardy. "How silly to be caught!" and she laughed and squeezed us all together in her arms. "Now, off you go!"

Crafers was a nearby village. We went there only on Sundays to attend church. The school was set apart from the town and totally surrounded by bush, so we existed in a separated and complete world, living the fantasies of the literature and the science we studied. No family to go home to. No real world to intrude upon our scholarly dreams. The subjects we excitedly read about were transported from the schoolroom to the dormitories with us. We became the very knights and queens we studied; acting on in fantasy our delight in the ideas we were discovering each day.

Those were the happiest years of my childhood.

Mount Lofty became a garden of heavenly delights; of Maid Marian and Robin Hood played out within a terrestrial Eden of lilacs and rhododendrons.

We galloped our 'horse fantasies' through forests of flowers and slept in tented dormitories, plotting against Kings and Prefects.

Nancy and Miss Hardy were the only mortals in that childhood time zone.

Those long, glass windows of the dormitory reach out across valleys of nostalgia. All that time seems beautiful - full of all the wonder and discovery that childhood can yield.

The Sound of His Truck

By C. Edgar MacLeod

I remember the sound of his truck. The whining motor straining as it climbed the hill to our house. To this day my chest tightens when I think about it. No matter what was going on everything stopped and little voices screamed, "He's home. Daddy's home. His truck is coming!" And little bodies and tiny feet scurried everywhere.

I was ten and Adrianne was nine, yet we screamed like wardens at our seven-year-old brother because he had not taken out the garbage, at the five-year-old twins because their clothes were scattered on the floor, at each other because we knew what was about to happen. He would soon come through the door and life would change, instantly. Arriving home after school all of our time was spent in frantic anticipation of what would happen. And something always happened.

The front door would open and he slammed into the room. His black, curly hair was soaking wet from working construction all day, a red bandana tied around his forehead did little to slow the stream of sweat running down his face and allowing his tee shirt to stick to his thick body. His countless tattoos were barely visible through the dirt and grime and his breath always smelled of beer.

I learned early that chores were critical and if the younger ones did not complete their list I'd hear, "You better damned well do them or make sure they do." It was his rule that retribution would follow and not just for one – but for all. He never demeaned one. When he started he went down the line – everyone got his or her shot – that lousy, vicious, hurtful, belittling, shot. When you don't know any better you get used to it. It was normal – for you.

Dinner was never pleasant. It was always met with anticipation, terrified anticipation. I could have survived on

117

crackers and water had I been given a choice. There was no laughing or telling of stories. There were no asking questions. There was no, well, anything. He demanded his supper and quiet. I mean absolute silence. We sat at the table, all ten of us. My mother at one end, he at the other, and the rest sprinkled along the sides and baby in the high chair. We ranged from fourteen months to ten years.

We all sat very quietly while he recited grace. When I think about it now, I find it ironic because the moment he finished the prayer, he looked up to start cursing and screaming about the day he had endured. Telling us how stupid our teachers were, about how we never did anything in the house, about how hard he worked to put food on the table and how we did not appreciate anything. How selfish we were which was why he couldn't get ahead, because of all of us. He ranted about the lack of work, the chafing between his legs from sweating all day, about his employees. "Those bastards keep trying to take advantage of me!" And it went on, and on, and on.

I don't ever remember being asked what I was doing in school, how my friends were or if I had any friends, or did I need help with anything. I only remember knowing that I had to be silent. And never question anything.

We were not allowed to speak at the table. And we could not drink any liquid with our meal. Milk was allowed after our dinner was completed. And, if we did not eat something on our plate – well – it was there on the table the next morning for our breakfast. We were to eat everything on our plate and not waste food. After all, our mother had taken the time to cook it, and he worked hard to buy it, and dammit, we were to eat it. Liver, spinach, carrots; whatever item happened to be unpalatable to a six-year-old did not matter. "You either eat it for dinner, or it will be your breakfast the next morning." We ate everything on our plates...oft times for breakfast.

One time, I was probably fourteen or fifteen; I must have said something snotty to him. I don't know what or why. To ask would make him become truly enraged. I do

118

remember we were having spaghetti and the pot of sauce was on the table. Without a second thought, he picked up that pot and threw it at me. I ducked and it hit the wall spraying the red sauce over the wall, the floor and the guns mounted in his prized gun rack.

I ran for my life. I ran so hard and so fast up the stairs until I tripped, banging my head and knees and crying as I slid under my bed. I heard my mother yelling at him to stop and not follow me. So he simply hit her. I was spared – I got away – she didn't and neither did the rest of the kids.

I stayed in my room, under the bed, shaking until I fell asleep. When I got up the next morning the sauce had dried like cement across the knotty pine walls, the floor and his guns. I scraped, cleaned and polished everything before I left for school. There was not a question in my mind - I knew it had to be done – by me – right then. With that penance completed I left for school and tried to clear my mind so I could try and learn something because in the end I always started the day as a "stupid, useless, son of a bitch".

I sit some evenings unsure why the dark, low whispers continue crowding my head. I have begged them to stop for so long but they are there; the memories are always there and sometimes they scream. They greedily take my few moments of peace and push me to revisit that chaotic hell that I survived so long ago.

My mother was artistic – a painter, seamstress, and writer. My father screamed and cursed and hit. She was incisively articulate and used words instead of physical force. With one sentence she could put my father in his place and he hated that. He could not win against her words so he used his fists. She learned quickly to keep her words to herself.

In later years he calmed down. He left the scotch in the cabinet and stopped his physical abuse. He was finally afraid, afraid of her leaving for good and his being left alone – all alone. She had become so good at shutting down and making herself invisible that he finally understood what he had done. She took advantage of his fear, became brave and used her words.

He was terrified of being alone and no one wanting him around. I know my mother died first to spite him. She could have survived quite nicely had he died first. She liked the silence and being able to enjoy reading, painting and writing. She knew he would not fare as well and did not care.

He never forgave his children and felt they had taken advantage of him all his life. Given that he would get up in the middle of a snow storm and drag one of his kids out of a snow bank or plow their driveway or give them money or bail them out of jail and take them home. Yet no thanks from them were ever enough – nothing was ever enough. He wanted love and admiration yet he never knew how to earn it. He expected all of us to be pleasers, doers, and a don't-make-waves kid. When we didn't respond exactly to his expectations he got angry – so very angry it is unfathomable.

He wanted unconditional love but did his best to push it away, beat it down and totally annihilate it. He always, always followed up the occasional nice word with a hurtful, demeaning remark. We could have cleaned the living room to Army specs but there always seemed to be that piece of lint or smidge of dust left on a table. "So really, you didn't do such a good job – did you?"

When my mother learned to become invisible I took her place and became caretaker. When she got sick, which she did often to be out of sight, he came to me to scream about the kids, the housecleaning or dinner. When he found a less than clean fork in the drawer he emptied the contents of the entire drawer, as well as the dish cabinet, into the sink for a total rewash and dry – then, right then, at that very moment. My sister and I would spend an entire evening rewashing, by hand, drying and putting away dishes from every cabinet. Then we could go to bed. We were ten and eleven years old.

I made excuses. Not because the others needed or deserved them, but because excuses kept him semi-calm. I tried reasoning then resorted to manipulation just so he didn't hate me and everyone else. It was an untenable

120

position. I thought it would keep life stable because he focused on me and on what I was doing instead of everyone else. He totally discounted his other children. How could he do that?

I made up stories as to why I was the only one – in his eyes – that ever amounted to anything. Why I was the favorite. If they only knew. If only they understood the fear, pain, and unbearable sadness that I carried each and every moment and which still haunts me today. I thought if he liked me maybe I could say things that might lighten the horror for the others. If he were calm they would be safe. We might all be safe. I gave up everything to make him and my mother love all of us. But I failed. And I bear the burden. I am the loser.

When my mother gave up and willed herself to die he was inconsolable. He had no coping skills. He had led such a fierce, unhappy life he had no tools with which to try and gain the love of his children. After spending his life pushing all of us away he said, "I don't give a shit one way or the other about what you think of me." But in his own hell he did. They felt no love for him – just fear - horrific, chest crushing fear.

He had no concept of what a hug, a kind word, a touch to the shoulder would do for them. And to this day, each of us relives the question, "Why didn't he love me? What did I do?" I cannot imagine the sorrow that burdens their hearts nor can they imagine the anguish that resides in my gut. It is too late for us to be whole – to be truly friendly or warm. We have each gone through the fire and survived, but we have not emerged unscathed. Our spouses, our children and our careers bear the scars of our early years.

We have not overcome the anger and jealousy, nor do we have the inclination to do so at this stage of our lives. We have gone separate ways and simply cordoned off those pieces of our lives where we are safe. We do not venture past those gates. We have married into families and formed some sort of reasonable relationships. Our own children have gone forth – perhaps not to our liking, but not bruised nor beaten.

I believe we would all love to gather – no spouses or children, and just hug each other. Admit, allow, and understand what we went through and forgive – forgive those actions of children – born of fear and rage and sadness – that we leveled upon each other. In my soul I am afraid it is only I that wish for it.

Our lives have changed; our needs are different. Each has their own history book of childhood and the part they chose or were assigned. They believe they have left that terror behind except during the dark hours when they can't sleep and they remember. When they chose not to remember they drink, or eat or rely on pills or mentally sing very loudly. They try to make that fearful noise go away. They pray and imagine it never happened.

But it still exists as that dark, low whisper in the bottom of our hearts. It makes them uncomfortable and they know not why. It makes them angry and they know not why. It brings on sadness that knows no boundary.

We are all we ever had – we did not acknowledge it at the time – but in the pit of our souls – we know. And we are too old, too proud, too tired and too afraid to go back and relive the terror.

Those of us who hear the dark, low whispers grieve - a paralyzing grief that no one understands. No one but the souls who grew up in that house could understand. The ones who were there when the grief was born and still carry the burden today.

Special Gifts

By Richard Katchmark

Being a competitive male drives me to rank even gifts I have received over a lifetime. There must be a number one gift. I am nearly sixty years old and married for thirty-eight years, helped produce three children, and have been blessed with four grandchildren. Considering the wealth of presents I have received for my birthday, Father's day, Christmas and occasionally for our wedding anniversary, the yield well exceeds three hundred. How can any one gift stand out as really special? Still, I have identified my number one and a close second.

It happened on my eighth grade graduation day. In my mother's words, "Next year you will attend Glassport High School and begin your journey to adulthood. You will need to get yourself out of bed and be on time for the earlier starting time." She presented me with a gift-wrapped clock radio for my bedroom.

That summer I didn't have to care about being awake for school, but I enjoyed going to bed at night. I spent long summer days running in the woods, playing baseball, or just pushing the limits as fourteen-year-olds do with getting into trouble. In the evening I retreated to my bedroom and with my number one gift radio, I listened to the Pittsburgh Pirates play baseball. During those warm summer nights of 1960 my bedroom was filled with the crack of the bat and imaginary dust of an exciting slide into home plate. The Pirates were driving hard to win a pennant. The City and our surrounding small towns were enthusiastic about the prospect of a World Series in Pittsburgh.

After listening to daily radio broadcasts of the games, I concocted a plan with my friends, Jerry and Carl, to attend a baseball game on Thursday night. By alluding to the fact that an adult would be with Jerry, Carl and me on this innocent trip, I got my mother's permission to go. I also neglected to tell her that the games would be a twilight doubleheader instead of the usual single game. Jerry and Carl secured parental consent by saying they were going to the game with me since I was considered the responsible kid in the neighborhood. Everyone knew that when my dad had died two summers before I assumed certain adult responsibilities in our home. Thinking back even today, I am surprised that our parents did not confront any of us as to who the adult was going to be.

Working all day Wednesday, I helped my brother Eddie on one of his home building projects. I told him we were going to the baseball game on Thursday night, and how I needed money. Thursday afternoon Ed paid me three dollars and asked, "Now how much money do you have?"

"Just the three dollars. The ticket costs a buck fifty and I need a dollar for street cars."

Eddie smiled, "You can't go to a Pirate game and not eat a hot dog and a bag of roasted peanuts."

He handed me an extra two dollars.

After riding two different streetcars, Jerry, Carl and I arrived at Forbes Field in the Oakland portion of the City of Pittsburgh. Three small-town kids out to enjoy the massive baseball park and see our beloved Pirate players close up. We purchased tickets in the right field stands so we would be closest to Roberto Clemente. The first game was exciting with Pittsburgh pulling out a late inning win. We spent the time between games at the refreshment stand and then sitting and eating in our seats. Brother Ed was right, a hot dog with brown mustard and a bag of freshly roasted peanuts were a great treat by themselves even before the second game started. The Pirates came back out and took a number of leads. We cheered and screamed with everyone else. Jerry loved to holler at the top of his lungs, "Arriba, Arriba" toward Roberto Clemente. The Chicago Cubs were tough competition that day and kept managing to tie up the game. At the end of nine innings it was tied at six to six. Finally in the bottom of the twelfth the Pirates scored and the ballpark

124

went wild. Everyone jumped up, clapping and hugging each other. From the announcer's booth Bob Prince waved his "green weenie" as a sign of two great baseball games won.

Outside of Forbes Field a congested sea of noisy people streamed out to the street. Being kids, we could squeeze around the adults until we got near the streetcar stop, where we waited with the crowd. I hollered out, "Is there a streetcar coming?"

I heard back, "No kid, the streetcars stopped running at midnight. It is now 1:15. The only way home is to walk or take one of these taxi cabs everyone is waiting for."

I had never in all my short life ridden in a taxi and neither had Jerry or Carl. We did know it took money to ride a taxi, and pooled our cash. No dollar bills, but we had almost three bucks in coins. We pushed along with everyone else until a cab pulled in front of us. We jumped in.

"Do you kids have money to hire this cab?"

"Yes," Carl chirped, "We have two dollars and eighty five cents."

"Where are you going?"

"Glassport," we said in unison.

"That's a long way, that $2.85 isn't going to get you there. Get out and let me take some more full fares. Then I will come back and get you, if you're still here."

Exiting the cab, I knew this was not a good situation. We moped around for an hour and considered calling our parents.

"I'll get killed," Carl said. "It's after two in the morning. I don't want to call them."

"I don't want to call either," added Jerry.

"I sure am not going to call my mother," I affirmed.

We waited. The crowd was nearly gone. A yellow cab tooted his horn. We ran over and found that the driver we talked to earlier had returned.

"Give me your $2.85 and I will drive until the money runs out. You will need to walk the rest of the way. Is that okay with you?"

"Yes," I acknowledged as we jumped in.

The money ran out quickly, and the driver informed us, "Your money is used up. We have driven eleven miles. You have about four miles to walk. I think you boys can make it."

We opened the door and Carl went to the curb immediately and sat down.

"Let's go Carl," I encouraged.

"No. I'm not moving."

"Why not?" I yelled.

Carl only pointed toward the cemeteries up ahead. Illuminated by dreary streetlights, their shadowy headstones spread out on both sides of the road.

"I can't walk through there." He pointed again.

"Carl, you have to walk with us so we can all get home. It's the only way."

He did not budge, so I continued, "I read that when a cemetery has a road through it, the spirits on one side can't cross over to the other side. If we keep our feet directly on the white highway center line nothing can touch us."

Jerry asked, "What book was that in?"

"One I didn't tell you about." I snapped back. "Let's go Carl."

Leading the way, I was sure to keep each foot on the centerline. Carl held the back of my belt and duplicated each of my steps. Jerry was not afraid to bring up the rear knowing full well I made up the ridiculous cemetery and spirit crap.

We cleared the graveyards and moved over to the sidewalk even though no cars were in sight.

We continued walking silently for over two miles and still there were no cars in sight. Finally I could see the Mansfield Bridge crossing over the Monongahela River. Our hometown was just across the bridge. Then six blocks, and we were home. I sensed now that we could easily make it.

However, as we arrived at the bridge, Carl stopped walking and balked, "I am not walking over that bridge."

Jerry tried to be encouraging, "Come on, Carl, this is easy. It is all concrete and solid. It holds up cars, it surely can hold us up."

126

"I am not walking over that bridge. I'm scared. I will wait for a car."

All three of us sat on the curb at the approach of the bridge.

I added, "Carl, this could be a long time sitting here. We have not seen a car since we got out of the cab. We may not see a car until morning."

Jerry piped up, "We can leave you here, Carl, and walk across the bridge. You can wait until morning."

"We are all sticking together, Jer, we are not leaving him." I turned toward Carl and said, "Carl, did anything happen when we walked along that white line through the cemeteries?"

"No."

"I promise you – nothing - will happen if we walk on the white line to cross this bridge. Are you ready?"

"Okay," he stammered.

We were back again in single file stepping on the highway white center line with Carl holding my belt. Thank goodness no cars came across the bridge.

The next six blocks were uneventful. Jerry left us as he walked down the steps to his house. I listened for the screen door to close, and Carl and I continued to Carl's house. We walked right past my house and eight more houses before we got there. Carl stepped onto the porch and went into the house.

I turned for home and realized that now I was alone. A dog barked or was it a hound? I wished my last book report hadn't been, "The Hound of the Baskervilles" by Arthur Conan Doyle. I ran down the street to my house and easily opened the unlocked front door. Its familiar loud squeak resounded in the three AM perfectly quiet house. My feet were half way up the stairs to my bedroom when the sting of a rawhide strap stiffened my shoulder blades. It hit a second time from the hallway above me accompanied by my mother's scream. "What are you doing out until three o'clock in the morning? You are getting into trouble and I know it." The strap landed a third time across my back as I reached the top of the steps. Without saying a word, I continued walking through my older brother's bedroom and into the bedroom I shared with my little brother. I knew my mother would not follow. I took off my jeans and threw them in disgust against the wall. My brother jerked and quickly sat up in bed. I told him it was nothing and to go back to sleep.

The word "NO" flashed big and white on the screen of my mind. No! The actions of the last few minutes will not ruin my wonderful evening at the baseball game. I continued to undress and lay on my side of the shared bed. Resting my hand on my radio, my mind relaxed. I could still smell the aroma of the baseball stadium, and see myself buying the hot dog and peanuts. I lingered in the memory of my second great gift. The money used to make the purchase. My older brother who never appeared to wake during my mother's screaming gave me that money. I thanked him in my mind for his special gift of dollar bills that made for a special evening of baseball. I withdrew my out-stretched hand and dozed off to sleep with the smell of hot dogs and roasted peanuts surrounding my bed.

To Rose Vivian Pelotte on Her Fifth Birthday

By May E. Shaw

A tiny maid came tripping in
With soft brown eyes and wavy hair
And this she said, this little maid,
With smiling face and modest air
In her own sweet and winsome way
I'm five, just five years old today!

And I'm to have a trolley ride
For mamma says that I may go
O I'm so glad, such lots of fun!
For Rachel's going, so's Aunt Bo
And Uncle John, and mamma too
We'll have such fun, I know, don't you?

Then Ma will make a birthday cake
And frost it with white on the top
And when it is done, one by one,
Over all sugar buttons will drop
'Twill taste so good, but ma will please
Save a nice piece for Aunt Louise

And mamma says that I shall go
Next fall to kindergarten too
And sing the songs and play the games
That other little children do,
I'm old enough to sing and play
For I am five, just five today -

Presented by Carol Woolfson and Betty Hyland:
their mother, Rose Vivian Pelotte,
was born June 29, 1895 in Fort Edward, New York

25413

By Lynda K. Jobman

25413 didn't look like the classic haunted house. For one thing, it was brand new in 1976 when we moved in. Like most homes in Florida, it was one level and built on a concrete slab. There were no creaky stairs, no basement, and no trees in the yard with branches to scratch at the windows. Except for the exterior color (peach) and some white brick around the windows and door, ours resembled every other house on the street.

On weekends, my parents, brother, and I would travel forty-five miles south from Miami, where our apartment was, to see the house as it was being built. My mother had chosen the floor plan, picked out the cabinets, tile and carpet, all neutral colors. I would stand in what would eventually be my room, still framed-in by wood, picturing where I was going to put my bed, desk and model horse collection. The excitement of moving, and not having to share a room with my brother anymore, took away any anxiety I might have felt about changing schools halfway through the fourth grade.

Princetonian Homes was not built on an Indian burial ground or an old cemetery, as the family lore goes, but on land once occupied by a lumber mill that closed in 1923 and before that a pine tree forest. There were about two hundred homes in the community, all brand new, with stucco walls and humble façades—a style that was part Mediterranean, part military housing.

I had just turned nine and my brother, Mark, was seven when we moved in. With so many children in the neighborhood, we spent most of our time riding bikes; exploring the Mound, a vast pile of construction debris a half-mile away; making forts out of plywood and empty appliance boxes; and playing in other kids' houses.

To hear my parents talk, our house was cursed. Looking

back, it's true that our moving in coincided with a sudden increase in emergency room visits. I sprained my finger in a wrestling match with Mark. He rode his bike into the side of a dumpster and broke his collar bone. Because there was still building going on in the neighborhood, between us we must have stepped on a dozen nails.

The second winter in the house we both developed fevers of 105 degrees and swollen lymph nodes. The ER doctor was amazed to discover that we were sick with two different diseases: Mark had the mumps; I had cat scratch fever. Just a few days earlier, our cat, Squeaky, had put her claw through my finger. I still have the scar.

"That damn cat was possessed," my stepfather will say to this day.

Animals are supposed to bark and hiss at evil spirits. Squeaky hissed at *us*. For no reason at all, she would launch herself at us with teeth and nails bared. She ripped the drywall in the laundry room and routinely used the carpet for her business instead of the litter box. Sometimes she bolted out the door, showing up a week later, meaner than ever, and pregnant.

Living in Florida, we were used to seeing bugs, but not in the house, or on our bodies. One day, as I was brushing my hair in the bathroom, I saw tiny insects crawling on the countertop, which turned out to be lice. Two shampoos with RID could not strip the eggs from my thick, shoulder length hair. Heartsick at the thought of shaving my head, my mother took the day off from work, and over several tedious hours that left my scalp aching, scraped her fingernails down every single strand of hair until not one egg was left.

Cockroaches will eat anything, even the inside of 8-tracks. We found this out after our neighbors—the Halls—returned some tapes they had borrowed. Wanting to listen to Fleetwood Mac, my mom inserted *Rumors* into the player. Nothing came out of the speakers but garbled sounds. I can remember her confused expression when she pulled the case out and discovered the ribbon was missing. Thinking that it had split somehow and was still inside, she shook the case upside down. Empty egg sacs and roach parts fell out.

We should have known better, but Squeaky was out of cat food one night, and it was easier to borrow some from the Halls who had two cats than to drive several miles to the nearest store. It was a scene right out of a horror movie when my mom opened what appeared to be a brand new box of Friskies and live roaches erupted out of it. With a yelp, she dropped the box on the kitchen floor. We squashed as many as we could, but the rest were too quick, vanishing under the cabinets. Some of them must have been females with eggs, because in no time at all we had a roach infestation.

For all the talk of evil spirits causing bad things to happen to us, my brother is the only one who saw a real ghost.

"One night I woke up and had a feeling that I wasn't alone in my room," he told me once. "Since I was on my stomach with my hands under my chest I couldn't look around, but I knew that someone or something was there.

"I must have counted silently to myself a million times, thinking, *On ten I'm going to turn over and look*, before actually moving. Leaning over me was a black figure that blocked out everything behind. It *whooshed* into Mom and Dad's bedroom. I was so scared, but I was more afraid it would hurt them, so I ran into their room and jumped on the bed to wake them up. Dad checked the whole house, but nobody was there."

After my stepfather lost his job in 1978, our financial situation became desperate. Though he found work, he was never able to hold a job for more than a few weeks at a time, a pattern that continued for years. Mom's salary as an assistant manager at a department store was not enough to cover all the bills.

The house fell into disrepair. Weeds grew up in the yard. Furniture did not move across the floor on its own, like it does in movies about poltergeists, but was carried out by my parents to be sold. A picture fell off the wall once, but that was because there were roaches bunched behind it. In a house as new and as small as ours there were not enough hiding places for all of them.

Daily life for me became unpredictable. I couldn't trust that there would be a dial tone when I picked up the telephone. Things that I had always counted on when I was younger, like lunch money and haircuts and new shoes when I outgrew my old ones, were no longer expected.

"Today was my twelfth birthday," I wrote in my diary on November 30, 1980. "Mom made a cake. I didn't get a present, but I had a fun time."

As much as possible, my mother tried to keep our spirits up. One night she made what she called Famous Mustard Clusters for dinner, slices of white bread with mustard and melted American cheese on top. It wasn't a real recipe; the ingredients were all that was left in the refrigerator. But Mark and I pretended that it was gourmet. We set the table and lit candles. What might have been a miserable meal for our family became a special occasion.

We only went hungry one night. Somehow my mother always managed to put something on the table, even if it was just lettuce and a few slices of tomato.

When I flip through my diaries of the time, I'm struck by how little I wrote of our problems. There are pages and pages with a single letter "N" on them, meaning Nothing Happened Today. Looking through photo albums of those years, everyone is smiling, especially at Christmas.

It was Mom's favorite holiday. She decorated every room in the house, insisted on a real tree when we couldn't afford one, and wrote letters to us from Santa. One Christmas Eve, she had us convinced that one of his elves had just been peeking at us through the window. Even after we were older, Mark and I pretended to believe, because it meant so much to her.

Broke as we were, my parents never cut back on presents, buying ten or more each for us, as if to make up for a whole year of going without. The child in me, who desired every single toy on her list, was at odds with the girl who knew from experience that come January the electricity or phone might be turned off because of over-spending in

December.

With all those toys it must have seemed like we were well off, because one day some kids whom we never identified broke into our house while we were away and stole my brother's entire Matchbox car collection and my stuffed animals. Just about every remaining toy we owned was on the living room floor, as if the thieves had played there for hours. The stolen toys were never recovered.

Mark and I were latchkey kids when we were in elementary school, but so were a lot of children we knew. As the oldest, I was responsible for watching my brother, who would run off to play after school, leaving me to straighten up, feed the dogs and let Squeaky and her kittens in so they could eat.

One night, when Mark left me to do all this myself, I lost my temper. I stomped onto the front porch with the intention of tracking him down and slammed the door behind me. Instead of closing with a satisfying *bang* the door bounced back open.

I've read that when an event is too traumatic the brain will somehow blank it out or allow only certain fragmented memories through. Even now, thirty years later, I can't recall exact details. I know one of Squeaky's kittens tried to squeeze under the door as I slammed it and the kitten's neck was broken. I know I killed it. But the only thing I can picture in my mind is the door bouncing back.

Mark said that he could hear me screaming three houses down. "I was at Tommy Thomas's house," he told me later. "I ran to you but the kitten was already dead."

I must have carried it from the front porch to my bed, though I don't recall picking it up. It released its bowels on the pink coverlet. A neighbor came to help, though I can't visualize his face, only his hands. He balled the kitten in some newspaper and took it away; I can still see the paw sticking up. I don't remember if my parents consoled me or were angry when they got home. All I remember is my mom saying, "I guess you won't be slamming any more doors." To this day I haven't.

Cursed or not, 25413 was home. Despite the awful things that happened there, I have fond memories too, of selling lemonade, jumping our skateboards over makeshift ramps, chasing down the ice cream truck, and playing Star Wars. I got my first ever love letter while living there. One day, Mark and I organized a bike race inspired by the Indianapolis 500. Though nobody actually finished all 500 laps around the block, we spent hours in the attempt.

"I feel so empty inside," I wrote December 19, 1980. "Mom and Dad say we're moving before or on the 10th of January."

Five years after moving in, we were evicted, leaving behind cat-clawed walls, a weedy yard, and the roaches. To this day, instead of blaming ourselves for what happened, we blame the house.

My brother once told me, "There was something creepy about that house that I picked up on as a kid, something not quite right."

My mother insisted for years that the house had changed my stepfather's personality, making it hard for him to get along with people and keep a job. "He was never the same after we moved in."

Charlie himself has said that the house was *no good*.

Was it really haunted? Was it built on graves? Was there an evil presence there that caused bad things to happen? Or was it just bad luck?

Some people believe that traumatic events can leave psychic imprints on a place, like an echo replaying itself over and over. I wonder who lives there now and if they see or feel strange things.

Have they experienced misfortune? Battled bugs? Seen Mark's phantom? Or heard a door slamming on its own? If 25413 wasn't haunted before we moved in, it is now, because of us. Because of me.

The War Years

By J.W. Harkin

On Monday, December 8, 1941, my fifth grade teacher, Mrs. Armstrong, asked if anybody could go home and get a radio so that we could listen to our President, Franklin Delano Roosevelt, declare war on Japan. I ran across the street and brought back a little table model radio. We listened to President Roosevelt describe the attack on Pearl Harbor as, "A day that will live in infamy."

The day before, when the Japanese attacked Pearl Harbor, I had been at Dad's gas station. It was a scary time. Uncle Toby had been drafted into the Army earlier that year, and Uncle Les was about to join the Navy. We were all very confident of the outcome. Those little Japs with buckteeth who couldn't pronounce the letter L would be no match for our All American Boys.

When the Second World War started so did gas rationing, and it killed the gas station business. While Dad and Mom tried to keep the gas station going, Dad looked for another job. For a while he worked nights at a foundry. When he came home from work, his clothes would contain zinc residue and small holes from the acid baths. He tried to get work in a defense plant, but could not produce a birth certificate. Finally, through an acquaintance, he went to work driving a furniture moving van for Grey Van Lines out of Chicago. I was ten or eleven at the time. Mom tried to keep the gas station going, but finally gave it up and found work in a defense plant.

At school we bought ten-cent war bond stamps weekly and pasted them in a little book. When we accumulated $18.75, we turned our book of stamps in for a $25.00 War Bond. We were told that War Bonds helped the war effort by buying war equipment. Later Jack Griffin and I were chosen to represent Prescott Grade School in a War Bond parade held in downtown Minneapolis. We rode in a Jeep that supposedly our school had bought for the Army with our war bonds.

Uncle Toby was drafted into the Army early. A missing finger and a mangled thumb on his right hand suffered in a childhood threshing machine accident, made no difference, the infantry needed men. Uncle Les joined the Navy. Gram, my Aunt Beverly, and her cousin Leatrice moved in with us.

Basic things became scarce. Our military had first priority on our country. Everyone was issued ration books. They contained coupons for gasoline, meat, sugar, shoes, and other things. If the stores had these items, you not only paid, but you surrendered ration coupons. Sugar was highly sought after for canning fruits. Dad bought a fifty-pound sack of black market sugar and hid it in an alcove over the gas station office. When Mom gave up the gas station, the sugar was hidden in our basement. I worried about getting caught and called a 'hoarder.'

Assembly lines that used to build cars now built tanks, airplanes, and jeeps. Major brands of cigarettes were hard to get. Lucky Strike, a favorite cigarette of many had been sold in a green package. Just after the war began Lucky Strike came out in a white package with the slogan, 'Lucky Strike Green has gone to War.' Silk stockings for women vanished. The silk was being used in parachutes.

One day a week was meatless. I think it was Tuesday, a weekday other than Friday, the day already declared meatless for Roman Catholics. We mixed crackers and oatmeal into hamburger to make it go further.

We were encouraged to grow as many vegetables as we could. Victory gardens popped up in almost every backyard. When the tomatoes got to about the size of baseballs, we would pluck a few, and instead of snowball fights, we'd have green tomato fights. The only difference was that instead of just being cold and wet when we got home we reeked of tomatoes.

Good coffee was very scarce. Coffee drinkers were forced to mix in chicory, a roasted southern plant root to

137

make the coffee go further. Some actually reused their coffee grounds.

Our public transportation, electric streetcar and bus system, in Minneapolis was excellent. Many people that worked downtown used the public transportation system rather than drive. If you worked at one of the defense plants outside the city, you carpooled or rode a bus. Carpool drivers were issued extra gas rationing coupons.

Because new tires were rationed we got our worn out tires recapped. The new tires were made of synthetic rubber, butyl. Butyl tires were not as flexible as rubber tires. When a car with butyl tires sat overnight, they would actually have a small flat spot where the tire rested on the road. When the car started to move you could hear a slap, slap, slap sound until the tire heated up and the flat spot returned to the natural arc of the tire. This was more noticeable in the winter.

Used oil from oil changes was collected by gas stations and sent in to local oil refineries to be cleaned and reused.

In addition to War Bond Drives, there were paper drives, and rubber and metal collections. We were going all out to win the war.

Duck, pheasant, and deer hunting seasons went by without many participants because gasoline was rationed and shotgun shells were hard to get.

Many churches and charitable organizations prepared Care Packages for England. Among other things they contained canned food, knitted scarves, gloves, and Afghans.

A friend of Dad's drove a cross-country furniture-moving van. Dad tried it and liked it—A life of freedom on the road. Mom gave up the gas station and began working in a defense plant that made projectiles for the Navy. An inspector, she insured that each projectile met very stringent specifications. She claimed that she had to be tough because, "One of these shells may save her brothers, Toby or Les's life."

When Gram began receiving allotments from Toby and Les, she along with Bev and Leatrice moved back to their duplex. While they were living in South East Minneapolis, Dad was on the road, and Mom was working in a defense plant, I became a latchkey kid. I would start dinner, peeling potatoes and putting them on the stove to cook so that we could eat when Mom got home.

Defense plants such as New Brighton, Northern Pump, and Rosemont sprung up around Minneapolis and St. Paul. They paid good money, operated three shifts with premium wages for the night shifts and provided lots of overtime. Men from rural communities flowed into the Twin Cities looking for and finding work, but finding a place to stay was more difficult. Some even "hot bunked"—same bed in use 24 hours a day.

Mom took in a boarder. He slept in my bedroom, and I slept on a daybed in the dining room. He was an older man, tall and slow speaking—a displaced farmer. I'm not sure how this went over with Dad, but I'm sure we needed the money. Dad was responsible for buying and maintaining his own semi-tractor. They were expensive. Before he could get one paid for it broke down, and he would have to get another.

We followed the war in Europe and the war in the Pacific closely. When H.V. Kaltenborne came on with the news, he would start with, "There's good news tonight," even in the worst of times. Edward R. Murrow began his news reports with, "This is London." His descriptions of the London blitz with the air raid alarms wailing and the crump, crump of falling bombs in the background were frightening.

We wrote to Toby and Les. Our class wrote letters that were given to servicemen that didn't receive any mail. Girls, young and old, became GI (Gentleman Infantry) pen pals. With the massive amount of letters being written and the space they required for transportation, a new letter was developed, V-Mail, V for victory. One sheet of paper that when folded became its own envelope. These were photographed and reels of tape transported instead of the actual letter. At their destination, the tape would be used to print the letters for distribution.

We had air raids and blackout drills. No unofficial outside movement was allowed. We covered our windows with cloth so that no light could be seen from the outside. Air Raid Wardens wearing metal helmets and official Air Raid Warden Arm bands monitored the efforts. A few people built their own underground air raid shelters stocking them with food and water. Our air raid shelter was our basement.

As the casualty lists lengthened, it became obvious that this was not going to be a short war. In the front windows of every home that had a son or husband in the war hung an 8" by 11" blue flag with a white star for each family service member. When a member was killed the flags were replaced with gold stars on white fields. Women with sons killed in the war were called gold star mothers.

Toby and Les survived. Toby, suffering from the effects of malaria, came back on leave just as the War in Europe ended—A skinny and sickly pale yellow version of himself. An infantryman he fought at Guadalcanal, where he was promoted to Sergeant. He said little about his experiences. He would crave a malted milk, but when he had one, he'd throw it up saying, "Too rich." He warned, "We're going to have trouble with the Russians. After we finish with the Japs, we should go after them." Toby was mustered out before the war in the Pacific was over.

Les flew in a slow moving Navy Catalina Bomber out of the Aleutians. He tells the story of his flying boat being hit by shrapnel from enemy gunfire while tracking a group of Japanese war ships. It began leaking fuel. During the long flight back to their base, they worried about having enough fuel to make it and the chance of a spark igniting the fuel fumes in the plane. A flying bomb he called it. They made it.

An Erickson cousin of my Mother's didn't make it. He was killed in the Battle of the Bulge. I served as a pallbearer at his funeral when his body was returned from overseas.

We learned early to hate the Nazis and the Japs. The stories of atrocities grew and became more horrible as the war years passed. When the Atomic Bombs were dropped on

Hiroshima and Nagasaki, we were overjoyed. If it saved one of our servicemen's lives, it was worth it regardless of the toll in Japanese civilians.

Water Balloons

By Brenda Kuhlman

Dad was throwing something in the trash, and he didn't want us to see. Joel and I hid behind our comic books, pretending not to notice. As soon as Dad left, Joel raced to the garbage can and looked inside. He fished out two tiny plastic packages. "Trojans," he squinted as he read.

"Quiet," I cautioned. Dad's heavy footsteps were returning.

Dad's face appeared before the rest of him as he peered around the corner. His dark eyebrows went way up high on his forehead when he noticed what twelve-year-old Joel had in his hand.

"Do you kids know what those are?"

Joel quickly dropped the packages on the table and walked away, shrugging.

Of course we knew what they were. In Bayside High, every teenage boy had a circular indentation on his back pocket from where a condom was stored, secured in a wallet. Ready if necessary.

"They're water balloons," I said. Dad grinned. I knew he'd ground me 'til middle age if I showed any knowledge of sex. He didn't know that Mom had explained her recent surgical procedure of having "her tubes tied."

"Yeah," Joel said. "You fill them up with water and throw 'em off the roof."

"Well, here," Dad said, offering us each a package. "Have a water balloon."

It was yucky and smelled like medicine when opened, but I dutifully ran it under the faucet. Problem was, it kept getting longer and longer as water filled it. Finally I tied it off and held it up.

"Put it in the freezer until we need it," Joel said. I hid it under a pile of freezer-burned hot dogs.

Months later, Nana came to town. She wasn't her normal cheerful self on account of a recurring toothache, a result of poor early nutrition and lack of dental care.

One day Joel and I sailed through the front door after school, throwing down our books and coats. We stopped in our tracks when we saw Nana. We stood for a long time and stared.

Nana was seventy-seven years old at the time. She was wearing her usual outfit: a cotton pink housecoat snapped shut over a polyester pantsuit. There was often a bottle of Anacin or Bufferin in her pocket. That day there was a new accessory in her hand: the frozen condom.

The water in the condom had frozen to the most unique shape. Regardless, she raised it gently to her cheek and sighed in satisfaction.

Nana's long gone, but that memory will live forever.

The Writers of Chantilly

F. CLIFTON BERRY, JR. writes feature articles and produces illustrated non-fiction books on defense and aerospace topics. He served in the U.S. Army as an airborne infantry officer, seeing ground combat in Vietnam. He and his family have lived in Northern Virginia since he retired from active duty to pursue a career in publishing as a magazine editor, feature writer, and book packager.

KAREN BROWN has lived a long life of trial and error, cause and effect, action and reaction, and has mostly learned not to make the same mistakes again. She has experienced joy and sorrow, success and failure, and has had the good fortune not to know when to quit. Quit what? Quit anything. If she wants it badly enough to start it, then she normally wants it badly enough to finish it. If not, she admits her mistake and moves on.

WILLIAM R. BYRNE is a Middle School Social Studies teacher, lives with his wife and two teenaged children in suburban northern Virginia. Modified Softball is an excerpt from his collection of short stories, *How Long Does It Take To Catch A Fish*?

DON COLLIER is a retired airline executive, has written for an airline trade magazine and various house organs. He is currently developing several novels. He draws from childhood experiences in Alabama and professional engagements in Alabama, Kansas, Florida, Georgia and the District of Columbia.

CATHARINE COOL was born in Malacca, Malaya of Australian parents. Educated in Australia she went on to graduate studies in London, married an American anthropologist and they traveled to Samoa to do research. During the next four decades she lived and worked throughout Asia, from the Philippines to Pakistan, sometimes as a teacher, always as mother, poet and artist. Since retiring to Virginia she has published two memoirs, *Vivid Air* and *Each In His Lonely Night,* and is now completing the third of her trilogy.

FREDERICK DOVE is an engineering consultant currently on contract to General Dynamics. He lives in Fairfax and enjoys bicycling, motorcycling and spending time with his only daughter and other family members.

MELANIE FLORENCE is currently teaching biology classes and labs at Dixie State College in St. George, Utah. Her short stories and poems have appeared in various anthologies as well as Dixie State College's literary journal, *The Southern Quill.*

MARY GANNON writes short fiction and has been published in *Mississippi Review*, *Catalyst,* and *Downstate Story.* Her full-length play, *Other Voyages on a City Street,* is a drama about working women and was produced in Chicago at the Playwrights Center Theater. She recently completed a novel, *The Sacred Street*, and a full-length drama about Washington, DC, *Beltway.*

MARY ELLEN GAVIN is a Story Teller who teaches Creative Writing and inspires new writers. She presently works as an Editor/Script Consultant in California.

J.W. HARKIN is a retired Navy Captain. His writings have appeared in *The Washington Post, The Retired Officer Magazine, and Unsent Letters: Writing as a way to Resolve and Renew* by Writers Digest's Walking Stick Press. When not creating short stories, he works on his memoirs—a diverse thirty years in the Navy.

DIANE HUNTER resides with her husband, Reuben, in Northern Virginia for the past 40 years. She is currently working on a collection of childhood memories and is delighted to share one of those moments in time in this anthology.

BETTY HYLAND spent her childhood summers at her grandmother's house in a small village in Upstate New York. Not just her Uncle Joe, but other relatives, friends, neighbors, and occasional unwelcome guests have appeared in the many stories she has written over the past thirty years. Some characters still pester to be included.

LYNDA K. JOBMAN writes essays and articles that have appeared in national newspapers and magazines. She lives in Virginia with her husband and sons.

RICHARD KATCHMARK works a day job to feed the family. He writes so that ideas and words inside him can have life on paper. He can't keep his mind shut. Six book length writings, two non-fiction and four fiction, plus two booklets of snippets have received life.

KENNEDY KELLY writes with characteristic Irish wryness: sometimes with a wink, sometimes with a sigh and often about the consequences of jumping class but snagging your cuff on the way over. In addition to her essays, she is also editor-in-chief of a magazine and publishes trade books. Far from the Long Island of her childhood, Kelly now lives in Oak Hill, Virginia and hides out in a cabin in Hedgesville, West Virginia.

BRENDA DAREFF KUHLMAN has been published in previous anthologies. She works for the Department of Social Services and writes part-time for *The Country Register* newspapers. Her favorite is short stories, though. She is a proud product of the New York City public school system and a tight-knit extended family, and it is from there - and her husband - that she gets her inspiration for writing.

C. EDGAR MACLEOD is a first-time published author who brings to life this revealing, and perhaps all too common, memory from childhood.

R. PATRICK-ALLISTER lives in Virginia with her husband of 26 years. She has two sons.

MAY E. SHAW was a neighbor of the Pelotte Family who penned the poem, *TO ROSE VIVIAN PELOTTE ON HER FIFTH BIRTHDAY*. She was inspired when Rose, the little girl next door, came to tell May about her fifth birthday plans. Carol Woolfson, daughter of Rose Vivian, has the 108-year-old, hand-written poem framed and in her home. It is a family treasure.

JOHN STIPA first began telling stories to his daughters at bedtime. It wasn't long before the keyboard became a portal to worlds not yet created, characters not yet brought to life, emotions not yet known to exist. If you turn back the cover and relax your mind, maybe he will take you to a place you've always wanted to go, protected by the veil of your imagination.

CAROL WOOLFSON was born and raised in Flushing, but spent summers in a village of 2,000 in upstate New York. These diverse experiences helped shape and balance her childhood. She now lives in California.

jd YOUNG is a writer whose last book, *Scarlett's Letters*, is filled with laughter and wry humor. Listed on Amazon, it boasts a five star review. This current offering takes us to the other side of humor.